PROBLEM-BASED LEARNING:
Welcome to the "Real World"

A Teaching Model for Adult Learners

Dr. Wendy J. Flint

Word Unlimited
Since 1985
Indio, California

PROBLEM-BASED LEARNING:
Welcome to the "Real World"

A Teaching Model for Adult Learners

USA ISBN 1-4196-7403-X

Word Unlimited
World Wide Web: www.experienceteaching.com
E-mail: doctorflint@yahoo.com

Printed in the United States of America

CONTENTS

Dedication

To my three children who pursued education and training and found their life purpose – Scott, a businessman; Todd, a paramedic-firefighter; and Tracy, an educator. You inspired me to find my purpose too.

Special Thanks

To the training team at Hewlett-Packard's Ink Jet Printing Division from 1991 to 1996, who changed my learning life forever.

Abstract

This book reviews some of the changes that have taken place in higher education in recent years that have been disrupting the traditional forms of curriculum design and course facilitation. According to the Office of Educational Research and Improvement, problem-based learning is a strategy choice for workplace trainers, instructional designers and educators because "in a society where change is constant and teamwork is a way of life at work, the lessons learned through involvement in problem-based learning are essential for students' career development." The characteristics of problem-based learning are explained and the theories that support problem-based learning are explored, including adult learning theory concepts of experiential and active learning. The teaching techniques and instructional activities used to design problem-based learning are case studies, simulations, and collaborative learning. There is an emphasis on the need to prepare the future workforce to meet the challenges of a global economy.

Forward

My desire to improve teaching methods in order to increase student success stems from my own struggles in education. I could not excel in learning in the 1950s and 60s, and no one knew why since there seemed to be a lot of "smarts" in my family. No matter how hard I studied or how much time I spent reading the textbook, I could only get a "D" or "C" on a test. I was 750 out of 950 when I graduated from high school. The essays or written homework assignments "saved me" and I was good at classroom discussion and oral presentations.

Looking back, I self-diagnosed my challenges as having attention deficit disorder (which prevented any effective test taking), dyslexia (reversing letters and numbers), poor eye vision, and an inability to recall – memorize.

At age 17, attempting to attend a state College in Ohio was a disaster. With all the activities to distract me, (surrounded by people and noise in the dormitory), I could not focus and once again, could not take tests with any success. I did well in literature, speech, and writing – but that did not help my overall grade point average. After one year, my parents decided to move from the East coast to the West coast and could no longer invest in my education.

In order to find some purpose in my life and to provide for myself, I joined the U.S. Navy at age 18 in 1968. To my surprise, I was third in a company of 80 in my course scores. The teaching methodology was different – more practical and more engaging. At a later time in my life, at age 28, I took an aptitude test for the Air National Guard and only missed 3 points in Electronics – achieving one of the highest test scores in the nation. I had no explanation for the recruiter except, "I just knew," regarding the answers.

I was placed in telecommunications and excelled at reading schematics and building PBX systems. My brother had demonstrated these same gifts participating at an earlier age in electronics. He never pursued college because the military had the technology courses in the 1960s that he wanted. I learned later that he did poorly in mainstream education also and had worse grades than mine. It seems we both had a different kind of intelligence that mainstream education could not assist.

In the 1970s, my husband and I were hired on the same day by Pacific Northwest Bell and sent to pole climbing school. He ended up in residential telecommunications and I was placed on a PBX team, much to the complaint of the men who served 20 years in "tip-and-ring" crews before they advanced to PBX. To the amazement of my boss, I would be given a box of equipment and cable, left in a business attic or storage room with schematics, and within 4 hours I would have the equipment built and running. Half expecting me to fail, they finally saw my value and sent me to PBX classes.

At age 43, I worked at Hewlett-Packard's Inkjet Printer division in the training department. I was required to attend soft skills workshops and technical classes. In their course instruction methods I was retaining skills and knowledge and developing a passion for learning. It was at Hewlett-Packard that I discovered adult principles of learning, action learning, learning styles, multiple intelligences, and problem-based learning. The "way" the trainers taught adults was working for me.

With my co-workers encouragement, at age 44, I found an adult learning theory university (Marylhurst University in West Linn, Oregon) and enrolled to earn a Bachelors' in Communications with a Specialization in Training and Development. I didn't have to take any tests but rather I proved my mastery of the subject through research, writing, oral presentations, portfolios, and collaborative projects. I was given a tutor in math to fill in the gaps developed during my public education. I also earned several credits through the documentation of my prior learning experiences.

I was able to attend school on the weekends and pay attention through classes that were several hours long. Why? Because I was engaged in problem-solving case studies and team activities. I was fully interacting with other students and learning from them as well as the instructor. The window of my brain opened up and knowledge poured in. I was now thirsty for learning and could not stop pursuing additional education.

Within ten years I received three degrees, worked in four different organizations, doubling my income with each degree. My PhD, awarded in 2004, reflected my life passion – a doctorate in Education with a specialization in Teaching and Learning. (Currently I am working on another degree – my MBA).

As a part time professor at a university and an instructor of management courses at a community college, I discovered other students who needed to learn in non-traditional ways. With an understanding of multiple intelligences and learning styles (See Appendix B, C, and D), I began to practice the concept of problem-based collaborative activities in the classroom that I used in corporate training programs. Students became more engaged and improved in their test scores. Several students would ask me to please share my teaching style with other professors because in my class they were "finally getting it" and enjoying learning.

The concept of learner-centered teaching techniques became my research project for my dissertation: "Faculty Development Toward a Learning College: Critical Reflection on Learner-centered Teaching Methods." The results were significant. Students who participated in the research were fully engaged and learning increased. Faculty who were involved in the research were convinced that they needed to incorporate more problem-based activities in their instruction and reduce the amount of time spent on lecture.

It is my hope that educators will apply the research and theories in this book to their instructional design and in the classroom so that a struggling student may awaken and discover his or her self-worth, gifts and talents; and so that all students will learn how to critically think and learn how to learn. May students enter their chosen profession with the confidence that they have been fully prepared for the real world.

Introduction

Problem-based learning is a learning strategy that incorporates specific instructional pre-planned activities, focused on a relevant learner problem. It also allows for the flexibility of the situation and the learners in the classroom. This course model has its foundation in the theories of humanistic, learner-centered, and problem-centered design approaches.

Problem-based learning, an instructional model based on constructivism and first practiced in medical universities, is the concept that learners construct their own understanding by relating concrete experience to existing knowledge where processes of collaboration and reflection are involved.

It is a method of learning in which students first encounter a problem, followed by a student-centered inquiry process. Both content and the process of learning are emphasized. Active discussion and analysis of problems and learning issues among students are essential to the process, enabling students to acquire and apply content knowledge and to learn and practice both individual and group communication skills.

Problem-based learning is "endorsed" by corporate training departments, health care organizations and college advisory boards, because it prepares the student for the real working world. It develops critical thinking skills and team skills that organizations need in their workforce for problem solving, decision making, quality control, and increased productivity.

Research for this book was conducted at College of the Desert, a community college in Palm Desert, California, a Hispanic Serving Institution. The research indicates that problem-based learning significantly impacts the degree of student engagement and learning. The research could have been conducted in junior high, high school, or universities because experiential learning is good for all ages that can critically think.

Community colleges, however, have a unique mission to not only prepare students to transfer to universities, but to also deliver a basic education to adults who are not prepared for college level work and to a large population of students being trained to enter or continue in the workforce. From computer technicians, to nurses, to accountants, to air conditioning repair technicians – community colleges have a huge responsibility to equip students for the 21st century employment pool.

The author and researcher, who is a corporate executive, adjunct business professor, professional workforce trainer, executive coach and organizational consultant, supports learner-centered strategies in education of all ages because:

1. There is growing research evidence that all students can learn at much higher levels in learning environments that are cooperative, collaborative, and supportive.
2. Diverse populations need diverse teaching and learning methods.
3. Problem-based learning is an effective method to assess student outcomes.
4. Learner-centered environments have been practiced in corporations for over twenty years with proven results through measurement of transfer of learning to practical application.

The literature reinforces the assumptions of the author, but the author also recognizes there is data indicating that teacher-centered strategies will always be considered a valuable part of education.

Ultimately, both are important, but unfortunately, learner-centered is minimal. Not because teachers don't want to implement the concept – but rather because they have not been taught how or they don't have the time for the instructional design.

Learner-centered concepts have been developing over five thousand years. They began in the 5th to 4th centuries B.C. with Confucius and Socrates. Two thousand years later in the seventeenth century Englishmen John Locke introduced experiential education.

"Another two hundred years passed before European educators Pestalozzi, Hegel, Herbart, and Froebel designed and popularized experience-based, learner-centered curricula and a century later, nineteenth century educator Colonel Francis Parker brought this method to America" (*Henson, 2003*). Henson (2003) notes that twentieth century Russian sociologist Lev Vygotsky, Swiss psychologist Jean Piaget, and American philosopher and educator John Dewey, shaped the existing learner-centered education into a program called constructivism. "Constructivism is a learner-centered educational theory that contends that to learn anything, each learner must construct his or her own understanding by tying new information to prior experiences."

Learner-centered is not new, but it has become more necessary with diverse learning populations. Flachmann (1994), author of Teaching in the 21st Century, wrote: "Good teaching is a journey rather than a destination. It's not like a subway stop where, once you are there, you can cease moving forward. Inertia is an insidiously powerful negative force in teaching – the urge to keep doing things the way we've done them for years. We have to resist the temptation to stay as we are; to rest at the bus stop."

Designing and incorporating problem-based activities and projects into course curriculum moves educators from good to great. The question of greatness is not based on the "happy sheet" evaluations that rank a teacher as having dynamic presentation skills or telling great stories (even though that is important); nor is it based on whether a minimum of 75% of students pass the class with a "C" or better. Rather, greatness is discovering methodologies that reach the learning style of that one student who does poorly at reading and memorization, but excels at writing essays and oral presentations. Greatness is when a student remembers the answer on the test because he or she learned it (not just memorized it) in a problem-based activity.

Super greatness is when students use the same critical thinking skills to solve problems in their next class, in their next job, or in the world.

CHAPTER 1. A Learning Strategy

Higher education institutions are evaluating alternative learning methods for the 21st century. Part-time versus full-time, work-based versus institution-based, face-to-face versus distance learning, to name a few (*Bridges, 2000*). These changes bring student experience and an informal curriculum that is increasingly diverse.

Problem-based learning, a sister of experiential learning and learning internships at the workplace, brings the real life work-based scenarios into the classroom to offer the practical application of the theory or content of the course objectives.

[handwritten: ABILITY TO IDENTIFY THE RIGHT PROBLEM]

Students, and the organizations hiring them, want education to be relevant to the real world they will work in. Managers want employees and new supervisors to come to them with critical thinking skills and the ability to solve problems. If students do not practice problem-solving in the classroom, how will they be prepared for the real world? If our teaching is not designed to lead to desirable learning outcomes, we are wasting our students' time and the valuable resources of the community.

"Even though many of today's complex issues are within the realm of student understanding, the skills needed to tackle these problems are often missing from instruction" (*PBL, San Diego State University, 2003*).

[handwritten marginal note: QUOTE – ONLY PLACE PROBLEMS ARE GIVEN TO YOU IS THE CLASSROOM. IN THE REAL WORLD YOU HAVE TO FIND THEM]

Characteristics of Problem-Based Learning

Many of the new methods of teaching and learning offer instructional activities by which students can gain experiences that enhance their self-knowledge. "Problem-based learning, an instructional model based on constructivism, is the concept that learners construct their own understanding by relating concrete experience to existing knowledge where processes of collaboration and reflection are involved (Office of Educational Research and Improvement, 1996)." It is the "how" the students construct their own understanding that learners carry into their future jobs.

To explain the process in simple terms – students learn in teams, using a combination of textbook knowledge, course room information (theory),

[handwritten: WICKED PROBLEMS]

Inductive

ADD
FIND THE PROBLEM

and past experiences to solve a problem. The team then reflects and presents on "how" the group came to their decision or solution.

Posner (2001) gives scientific support for problem-based learning. He notes that "a crucial determinant of learning is students' thinking or cognitive processing, and this processing is directly influenced by the kind of tasks in which students actually engage."

In problem-based learning, students are presented with a loosely structured problem – one that has no obvious solution and for which problem-solvers cannot be certain they have the right answer. The problem must be content relevant and represent a real situation faced by an individual, group, company, or community. According to Savoie & Hughes (1994), solving the problem takes students through the following processes:

1. Engagement. Problem-based learning requires students to self-direct their search for a solution, often by assuming the role of a key actor in the problem situation.

2. Inquiry. Students brainstorm with others and gather information from multiple sources, including textbook and course materials.

3. Solution Building. Students work in teams discussing alternatives and examining possible solutions. often using probing questions provided by the instructor.

4. Presentation of Findings. Students write plans, reports, and other forms of work documentation to include in their portfolios (or students present their findings back to the class; or both).

5. Debriefing and Reflection. Students share information, opinions, and ideas with others based on what they have learned through the experience.

6. Instructor Feedback. The instructor shares feedback using his or her expertise to enhance the solution or redefine the process.

Problem-based learning is a strategy choice for educators because "in a society where change is constant and teamwork is a way of life at work, the lessons learned through involvement in problem-based learning are essential for students' career development" (Office of Educational Research and Improvement, 1996).

Wicked problems ⇒ no solution
only make better or worse

The outcomes of student-centered learning are that students learn how to:
1. Solve complex problems. *EFFECTIVELY &*
2. Evaluate resources. *EFFICIENTLY*
3. Work in teams effectively.
4. Communicate clearly and concisely (*Harper and Levine, 2002*).

There are many teaching strategies that when facilitated properly can increase student engagement, student learning, and transfer of learning. A variety of instructional strategies in the classroom help meet the needs of the diverse population of multiple intelligences and learning styles.

Instructional activities can include rubrics for self-evaluation of learning, collaborative learning projects, web research, role plays, case studies, and team problem solving.

Problem-based learning incorporates many of these activities into one process that is a highly effective method for encouraging students to use critical thinking skills in real world scenarios. The teacher becomes a facilitator of learning rather than a lecturer. Problem-based learning also provides an opportunity for students to identify with real work situations.

Typically five to eight students work collaboratively in a group. Active discussion and analysis of problems among students enable students to:
1. Learn from each other.
2. Apply content knowledge to a practical real world problem.
3. Learn and practice both individual and group communication skills.
4. Evaluate the learning and discovery process they used to achieve their goals and solve the problem.

Most educators agree that an essential goal of education is the development of students who are effective problem solvers for the information literacy age and many reports, such as the National SCANS (*Survey of Necessary and Comprehensive Skills*) and Goals2000 documents, recommend problem-based learning instruction (*Barrows, 2003*).

Managers want employees and new supervisors to come to their organizations with critical thinking skills and the ability to solve problems. Hospitals want doctors who can patient problem-solve using evidence-based evaluation, not just recall medical facts. Companies want engineers who can improve existing concepts or invent new products.

Research indicates that critical thinking and problem solving skills are not typically addressed in the classroom and that 85% of teacher questions are at the recall or simple comprehension level (*Barrows, 2003*).

The facilitator of a problem-based process evaluates if the learner can combine precious knowledge and experience, with new knowledge recently acquired in the classroom, and apply it to a real-life problem that will more than likely occur in the future.

For example, in the research for this book, during a pilot test of the project and surveys, a manufacturing simulation was facilitated in a business class. Prior to the simulation, the class was instructed in the use of Total Quality Management (TQM) using problem-solving and process evaluation tools. The simulation was designed to have work problems that are similar to a real world company. The students, working in teams, identified the problems and proposed solutions using the TQM tools.

Rather than just studying the theory of TQM, students were able to work on a real world problem. The experience will be applicable in their future vocations – whether engineers, doctors, supervisors, or waste management specialists. Problem-solving in teams is an expected skill that students will be required to achieve in future organizations wherever they are employed.

Cognitive psychology – the main stream of educational psychology in the last decade – has taught us that a student is not an empty vessel waiting to be filled with new knowledge. Learning is seen as an active process of constructing and reconstructing knowledge and problem-based learning is an approach consistent with these findings (*Perrenet, 2000*).

The greatest challenge of problem-based learning is how it redefines the teacher-as-sage role. The teacher has a variety of responsibilities, including curriculum designer, facilitator, assessor, and evaluator – none of which includes providing content or information to the students.

As curriculum designer they write problems that reflect real world issues. As a facilitator, they ask challenging questions. Teachers only become content experts when approached by the students or to clarify confusing concepts (*Harper-Marinick and Levine, 2002*).

As an assessor of learning, teachers may use traditional tests to assess content acquisition, but should use observation and group discussion to evaluate what the students gained from the experience, their ability to solve problems, effective teamwork, or clear communication (*Harper-Marinick and Levine, 2002*).

"Problem-based learning is an educational method which is learner-centered and in which the teacher is the facilitator of the process rather than the source of knowledge imparted to the students. Problems are the tools of learning, and students are participants rather than passive recipients of their learning" (*Limerick, B. and Clarke, J., 1997*).

The Office of Educational Research and Improvement noted a year prior: "In a society where change is constant and teamwork is a way of life at work, the lessons learned through involvement in problem-based learning are essential for students' career development" (*OERI, 1996*).

There are time constraints to consider with problem-based learning. Short class times do not allow for problem solving activities (projects outside of the classroom are recommended) and time must be spent in pre-class planning of instructional activities that align with student learning outcomes. Teachers who consider problem-based learning as a new approach need to start small and convert only a part of their course design. It will be an easier transition for those that have already incorporated cooperative learning or classroom assessment techniques in the course.

Organizing small group discussions is a good place to start. Problem-based learning also aligns with the teaching strategy models of experiential, collaborative, and group discussion (*Davis, 2001*).

Finkel and Monk (1983) proposed that if teachers cannot take the radical step of letting go of teacher-centered learning, then begin in small steps. They suggest that the teachers distribute their polished lectures in advance and instruct students to read them as preparation for class (*Finkel and Monk, 1983*). Students can bring prepared questions for the basis of discussion, or the students can work collaboratively in class to answer the questions.

Problem–based learning provides a method (the how) for teaching a learning outcome and an opportunity to assess if the learning has transferred. As a teacher evaluates his or her course objectives or learning outcomes, several will stand out as good "candidates" for problem-based learning.

If a learning objective states that students will be able to evaluate, practice, demonstrate, or communicate a specific skill or topic, the teacher can design an activity where students work in teams to solve a problem or answer questions to a teacher-designed or student-designed case study that ensure there will be opportunity to evaluate, communicate, practice, and demonstrate.

In problem-based learning, the role of the teacher changes from expert to helper. More than any other instructional strategy, problem-based learning forces a teacher to become a facilitator of learning, rather than an expert. "Students who are ingrained with these skills are well prepared for occupations which rarely have a supervisor who has time, inclination, or knowledge to tell the worker what to do. They are well prepared for the explosion of knowledge which gluts the world today" (*Davis, 2001*).

Chapter 2. A Learning College

The primary role of community college faculty is first to teach, rather than publish, so it is assumed that student learning is the primary focus.

If that is the case, then why are new concepts of faculty development being evaluated and college programs being reviewed? Perhaps because in the past, college faculty development focused on faculty as teachers (course design, presentation and student interaction), faculty as scholars and professionals, and faculty as individuals (wellness or interpersonal skills) (*George, 2000; Vaughan, 2000*).

What has not been offered to a greater degree is faculty as assessors, faculty as writers of student outcomes, faculty as quality assurance evaluators for improved learning, and faculty as leaders. Colleges moving in this direction are referred to as "learning colleges."

The need for developing learning colleges with learner-centered classrooms, has emerged primarily because of the demand put upon community colleges to respond to the local and global community regarding the preparation of a 21st century workforce. *INCORPORATE INTO OVERVIEW*

This workforce needs to know how to work in teams, make leadership decisions, problem-solve, manage change, think critically, and understand new technologies faster than the previous generation.

In addition, there are the pressures of state and regional accreditation agency requirements for system-wide output improvements in basic skills, course completion rates, graduation rates, transfer rates, and economic development.

In June 2002, the Accrediting Commission for Western Association of Schools and Colleges (WASC) approved new accrediting standards which went into effect for academic year 2003–2004. Those standards include writing student learning outcomes for all curriculums. Assessing those outcomes in the classroom will also be expected.

One of the most profound documents regarding education and our nation, written in April 1983, was titled *A Nation at Risk*.

Concern for the nation remaining economically competitive was one of the drivers toward teaching and learning reform. The report stated that even though a million and a half new workers enter the economy each year from our schools and colleges, the adults currently working today will still make up about seventy-five percent of the workforce in the year 2000 and beyond.

These workers will need further education and retraining. Most states have determined that it is the mission of community colleges to address the academic, continuing education, technology, and training needs of this century's workforce.

Add to this the severe problem of racial inequality in education. "The racial gap in academic achievement is an educational crisis and racial inequality is America's great unfinished business" (*Thernstrom and Thernstrom, 2003*).

Educational reforms have been implemented to address the demands of the new economy and diverse communities. Whatever the reform, the philosophy that continues to be the central theme, is the development of "learner-centered" or "learning colleges."

The 21st century educational principles of reform are all based on the assumption that improvements will occur only when the system is redesigned with the primary focus on the learner (*Wagner, 1993*).

Wagner (1993) defines a learner-centered program as "one in which the learner, no matter what age, is actively involved in the planning and evaluation processes as well as the learning process."

Following the Nation at Risk report, the National Institute of Education (1989) issued the "Involvement in Learning" report that called for increased emphasis on undergraduate teaching and learning, concluding: "Institutions should be accountable not only for stating their expectations and standards but for assessing the degree to which those ends have been met. They should make a conscientious effort to acquire and use better information about student learning, the effects of courses, and the impact of programs."

Learn how to learn
& be a systems thinker
Learn how to find problems

Diversity

With the need to accommodate the diversity of experiences and the wide range of cultures and learning styles, community college faculty are faced with new demands, often with little preparation or development to respond to the challenges.

"The premise of 'one teaching style fits all,' which is attributed to a teacher-centered instructional approach, is not working for a growing number of diverse, student populations" (*Brown, 2003*).

When teaching styles conflict with students' learning styles, the result is limited learning or worse – no learning. High school graduates are not entering college and the workforce with the skills they need to compete in a changing economy.

A report by the National Center for Education Statistics found that 42% of entering freshmen at public two-year colleges and 20% of entering freshmen at four-year public institutions enrolled in at least one remedial course in 2000. That percentage has been increasing every year according to the U.S. Department of Education.

Barr and Tagg (1995) note that colleges have aimed to provide access to historically under-represented groups such as African Americans and Hispanics, but "mere access hasn't served students well." They propose that the "goal for under-represented students (and all students) becomes not simply access but *success.*"

What do Barr and Tagg (1995) mean by success? "The achievement of overall student educational objectives such as earning a degree, persistence in school, and learning the 'right' things – the skills and knowledge that will help students to achieve their goals in work and life."

Students differ from course to course and from student to student within a given course. Because of demographic differences, students bring different feelings, relevant experiences, and prior knowledge to different courses (*Fink, 2003*).

The challenge is for teachers to know how to gather information about the characteristics of students to make decisions about how courses should be facilitated for maximum learning experiences.

The Paradigm Shift

Barr and Tagg (1995) refer to the existing paradigm that governs colleges as: "A college is an institution that exists to provide instruction".

In California community colleges, 45% of first-time fall students do not return in the spring and it takes an average of six years for a student to earn an associate's (AA) degree. "Educators are always surprised to hear this and the reason for this lack of outcomes knowledge is profoundly simple: under the Instruction Paradigm, student outcomes are simply irrelevant to the successful functioning and funding of a college" (*Barr and Tagg, 1995*).

Most faculty evaluation programs evaluate whether or not an instructor is organized, covers the appropriate material, knows the subject matter, and whether or not they respect their students' questions and comments. "Rarely does evaluation of faculty raise the issue of whether students are learning, let alone demand evidence of learning or provide for its reward"(*Ibid.*)

Maryellen Weimer (2002), author of Learner-Centered Teaching, is the former Associate Director of the *National Center on Postsecondary Teaching, Learning and Assessment*, a five-year U.S. Department of Education research and development center.

In 1994, she returned to the classroom as a full-time faculty member after thirteen years in administration and research to implement some of her discoveries.

She found over the years that education makes students dependent learners rather than independent critical thinkers – depending on the teacher to identify what needs to be learned, to prescribe the learning methods, and finally to assess what and how well they have learned" (*Weimer, 2002*).

Barr and Tagg (1995) support the theory of identifying teaching and learning structures that create climates for learning. They support learning that shapes knowledge individually (as mediated by personal experience) and makes learning student-centered. It teaches students how to learn as much as it teaches what to learn.

Barr and Tagg (1995) describe faculty as "instructional designers who put together challenging and complex learning experiences and then create environments that empower students to accomplish the goals."

Community college educators throughout the nation are devoted first and foremost to teaching and learning. Student learning has always been a theory in the hearts of teachers, yet teachers have been constrained by a system that is sometimes at cross-purposes.

"To build the colleges we need for the 21st century – to put our minds where our hearts are, and rejoin acts with beliefs – we must consciously reject the Instruction Paradigm and restructure what we do on the basis of the Learning Paradigm" (*Ibid.*).

Business and Industry

The Accrediting Commission for Community and Junior Colleges (ACCJC) Western Association of Schools and Colleges (WASC) list as a standard in their 2002 Accreditation Standards: "students completing vocational and occupational certificates and degrees must demonstrate technical and professional competencies that meet employment standards."

The Western Interstate Commission for Higher Education's Office of Research and Policy Analysis (1993) (after two years of research) concluded, "Higher education must prepare to meet aggressively the challenges posed by rapid changes in the economic structure and character in our society" *(Wagner)*. The report urged states to develop a statewide vision for higher education, embodied in a strategic agenda.

Faculty who are recruited from the business sector, who serve in internships, or who use their sabbaticals to "explore" real life fields of study, understand the need for a learning college to manage the challenges and changes.

Learner-centered strategies help prepare students for the real working world. The learner-centered methodologies used and tested by training organizations in major companies have proven results of increased transfer of learning - the ability to transfer knowledge or skill from one context to another or to a job (*Aspy et al., 1993, Gates, & Cooksey, 1998, Mila & Sanmarti, 1999, and Forman, 2002*).

Learner-centered training programs have also given employees additional necessary skills of team building, problem solving, decision making, risk taking, and effective communications. Understandings of "the world of work," of the way businesses function, and of how knowledge can be applied in these settings (as well as competence in the use of information technology) are increasingly becoming a necessary part of 21st century college curriculum (*Bridges, 2000*).

Post-secondary education and training has become an essential requirement for a steadily increasing percentage of jobs. According to the Bureau of Labor Statistics, 80% of the fastest-growing jobs in the United States require some sort of higher education after high school, and many of these jobs require a strong foundation in math and science.

A study done in 1989 revealed that employers deliver learning to more people than does the entire U.S. higher-education system (*Merriam & Caffarella, 1991*).

These non-educational organizations have played an increasingly larger role in adult education to meet 21st century workplace needs in both the private and public sector. The training techniques they have practiced and evaluated over the past fifteen years can benefit a learner-centered college institution (*O'Banion, 1997*).

Learner-centered environments defined by Knowles (1980) for adult learners are an important factor for the transfer of learning. Transfer takes place when existing knowledge, abilities and skills assist us in the performance of new tasks or affect the next step in the learning process. Often, what is learned in the classroom is not transferred until the student successfully applies or practices the learning in a new or work situation. Transfer of learning occurs when the learning in one context or with one set of materials impacts the performance in another context or with other related materials (*Mila & Sanmarti, 1999*).[1]

Consequently, the end goals of education or training are not achieved unless transfer occurs. Community colleges are being asked by legislators to determine what students need to learn and assess and measure if students are learning. Business and industry training has been required to deliver and measure training and education for over twenty years. As a result, new concepts and techniques have developed for increased learning.

These concepts and techniques have come together in powerful model called "problem-based learning."

1 Can we assume DHA students have an healthcare background.

Ability to create new knowledge and synthesize across copi

Chapter 3. The New Role of Educators

"In the 21st century, the community colleges' success will continue to depend on its ability to respond to a changing environment" (*Vaughn, 2000*).

The external factors are redefining what a teacher is. The role of the educator in a learning college is no longer one of teacher, expert, lecturer, or even a transmitter of knowledge. The new role in the 21st century is guide, director, or a facilitator of student learning.

As community college faculty members of the1960s and 1970s retire, community colleges will recruit new teachers in a highly competitive market. Faculty members will be expected to have a command of technology to the extent needed to teach their courses effectively. Teachers will be more likely to use a variety of teaching methods in addition to lecture, to help facilitate the learning of students who may have diverse ways of assimilating knowledge (*Vaughan, 2000*).

Halpern and Associates (1994) view the role of the educator in terms of the skills and strategies of thinking that must be addressed during instruction, emphasizing that critical thinking, problem solving, decision making, and creative thinking are not separate areas; rather they are all aspects of thoughtfulness, or sets of related and overlapping skills.

They note that in addition to learning these skills and how to use them in specific courses and disciplines, "educators will need to help students transfer their critical thinking skills to other academic contexts and to learn to apply them to their everyday lives."

Increasing numbers of faculty recognize that they are the "movers and shakers" of quality student outcomes, improved student learning, developers of the assessment process, implementers of strategic plans for diversity, and promoters of new technology.

As these responsibilities increase, the demand for new incentives and professional development will increase. Higher education administrations will need to be proactive in their plans to implement creative staff development models.

The problem is, how is this guidance best provided and how will it be done with limited resources and in some states, with extreme budget cuts? Faculty are concerned about increased workloads to achieve aggressive learning, assessment, and accreditation goals with reduced resources.

According to the California Community College Council for Staff Development and Community College League of California (2003), the learning college trends and curriculum revision for student learning outcomes will require the state and community colleges to devote funds to professional and organizational development programs.

Teacher as Facilitator

The transition from teaching the entire group, to meeting individual learner needs involves an understanding of learner college principles and learner-centered concepts.

Learner-centered environments do not focus on how teachers teach but rather focus on how students learn. The teacher is a facilitator of learning – a guide or director. Faculty facilitates and guide learning without contributing directly to the solution of the problem or being the primary source of information.

Faculty listens carefully, respond, and use questions to explore and stimulate students' thinking (*Mennin, et al, 2003*). Richart (2000), referring to Chickering and Gamson (1991), in their well-known article *Seven Principles for Good Practices in Undergraduate Education*, reminds us that "good practice":

1. Encourages student/faculty contact.
2. Encourages cooperation among students.
3. Encourages active learning.
4. Gives prompt feedback.
5. Emphasizes time on task.
6. Communicates high expectations.
7. Respects diverse talents and ways of learning.

All of these practices can be both teacher-centered and learner-centered, depending on the degree to which the teacher directs his or her own expertise in these practices or allows the students to develop their own goals and guidelines.

Instead of focusing on content initially, educators should first consider their students' needs, prior knowledge, talents, interests, social orientations, linguistic abilities, and cultures (*Brown, D., 2003*).

After considering these factors, teachers will understand what they should teach and which content their students can learn and benefit from. Focusing on how students learn means focusing on research on student learning styles, multiple intelligences, and the experiences of the students being taught (*Richart, 2000*). SMORGASBORG

The role of the educator in a learning college is not one of teacher, expert, lecturer, or even a transmitter of knowledge, but rather a person that promotes intellectual discoveries. The new role is a teacher that plans instructional strategies and classroom assessments to monitor and assist students in learning before they ever take the final exam.

Halpern and Associates (1994) note that students need to be able to transfer their critical thinking skills to other academic contexts and learn to apply them to their everyday lives. Learner-centered principles and methods in the classroom (or assignments outside the classroom) help students achieve these goals.

Faculty Development

Professionals in all trades must be willing to critically reflect on their own practices and hold their performance and effectiveness up to other best practices for review and evaluation.

Quality assurance means being willing to continuously improve a process or a task and continuously learn new ways of doing things. The concept of quality improvement has been incorporated into higher education for the past fifteen years, yet colleges have progressed at a very slow rate (*Luna & Cullen, 1995*). Quality improvement cannot take place without the empowerment and development of college faculty to understand their role in the process of institution improvement.

With student populations becoming more diverse (diverse ages, diverse ethnicities and cultures, diverse learning styles, and diverse reasons for attending college) faculty will need to take additional time for their own life-long learning to adapt to the changing community and global demands.

Colleges and universities are being encouraged to focus on *how students learn*, thus engaging in an active educational agenda to enhance such learning.

Focusing on how students learn also means conducting learner assessment in course instruction to evaluate the individual learner and the learning process. Educators across the nation have a growing awareness and concern that they need more skills to guide students through this learning process and take advantage of opportunities for self-improvement.

The Mid-continent Regional Educational Laboratory asked focus groups of teachers about the types of challenges they currently face in their classrooms, and what they needed to meet those challenges. The majority stated that it was "impossible for them to meet the demands of integrating learner-centered teaching methods, alternative assessment methods, strategies for dealing with the needs of diverse students, and methods for making better use of technologies in their classrooms - unless they were provided with guidance in how to do so" (*Wagner, 1993*).

Faculty development in teaching and learning is not a new concept. Twenty-five years ago (in the 1970s), Jerry Gaff targeted 200 campuses to identify and evaluate teaching improvement programs funded by federal and foundation agencies.

He titled his work *Toward Faculty Renewal* because the issue of the 1970s was "how to keep a now largely middle-aged faculty educationally alive and growing during the next two to three decades" (*Cross, 2001*).

Today, the middle-aged faculty of the 1970s are retiring, a new generation is taking their place, and the attitude regarding teaching improvement has changed. "The goal is far more ambitious – and more respectful – than keeping faculty 'educationally alive.'" (*Ibid.*) The approach today is to solicit the cooperation, collaboration, and participation of faculty and to offer services and resources in campus-wide efforts to improve teaching and learning.

Weimer (2002) warns that faculty resistance is all but a guaranteed response to learner-centered teaching. Resistance, according to Weimer, is based on the increased amount of work for faculty "who now face complex instructional design issues."

Additionally, some colleagues resist because they are concerned about what these approaches do to diminish the amount of content in course and they have legitimate questions and concerns. The priority is to determine the best learning practices for today's students, then research practical ways to implement these concepts and evaluating funding resources to make it happen.

Not all faculty resist learner-centered approaches. Angelo and Cross (1993) note that "when faculty collaborate with other teachers or with students in assessing student learning, they often experience synergy" and that "participating teachers often remark on the personal satisfaction they feel in working with colleagues and students toward the shared goal of improving learning."

Teachers become facilitators of learning (rather than lecturers and test administrators) and students become self-directed in their learning as they learn how to evaluate their own learning. With this kind of energy and satisfaction in the learning environment, teachers and students grow together.

Higher education teachers will be reluctant to change set patterns of thinking and behavior if they are not convinced that it is essential to do so, and rightfully so. This process of shifting a paradigm of thinking is called "transformative learning." Through dialogue, "faculty are guided to voice and examine their assumptions, expectations, and feelings about teaching, knowledge, and learning to clarify their beliefs and to identify gaps, flaws, and discrepancies in the belief system, perhaps opening it to revision" (*Vella, 2004*).

"We need better teaching and learning in college, but not because it is bad. The case for improved practice rests on a different set of premises, those that involve the changing realities of higher education and that offer opportunities as well as contain threats" (*Menges, Weimer & Associations, 1996*).

Faculty development has become urgent not because of poor teachers, but because of external factors, such as diversity of learners, diversity of learning styles, globalization, and a changing and aging workforce. Yet, with faculty adapting to multiple changes occurring within their community and educational system, it is not an easy task for them to find the time to initiate or participate in their own development.

Teacher-centered Advocates

Opponents of learner-centered strategies and advocates of teacher-centered pedagogy argue that students in basic skills classes thrive in a more teacher-controlled environment where comprehension or critical thinking is not required (*Smerdon, et al, 1999*).

It is expected that not all faculty will be in agreement with the learner-centered concepts. Smerdon (1999) also points out that teacher-centered curriculum already lend itself to teaching to standardized testing.

Other teacher-centered researchers have noted that students with lower academic abilities may thrive with structured curriculum and direct expert assistance (*Reyes, 1991; Delpit, 1995*).

Chall (2000) argues that education should move back to teacher-centered practices, especially with underrepresented students. She points out that "the traditional approach makes the objectives and tasks systematic and in order of difficulty."

More recent research by Norman (2003) found that there was no conclusive evidence that demonstrates students (English language learners) have a particular preference on whether they are taught under the teacher-centered or learner-centered approach and that "both teacher-centered and learner-centered approaches had a positive and significant impact on adult students."

Some teaching techniques can appear to be learner-centered, but are in fact a combination of both. For example, giving students a "rubric" with guidelines for success is learner-centered because students are responsible to monitor their own requirements, but teacher-centered because the teacher pre-selected the guidelines.

A learner-centered technique example would be to have the students propose the standards in teams; come to a group consensus to finalize the standards, with the teacher adding expertise in the "gap" when required.

The difference in this later scenario is, the students learn and practice collaboration, critical thinking, measurement standards, decision-making, presentation skills, debate, and goal setting, while committing buy-in to their own action plan.

Faculty who have been mentored in a learner-centered approach are positive about the concept and enjoyed the student engagement – but most have noted that they would need ongoing faculty development, mentoring, and sharing of best practices to incorporate learning-centered activities or problem-based learning into their existing course design. Large colleges have "learning centers" for faculty that offer professional support. Small to mid-size colleges often lack the resources to assist faculty in this paradigm shift.

Chapter 4. Rationale for Problem-based Learning

There are three major reasons that support problem-based learning as an optimal choice in a teaching method. It provides opportunity for student assessment of learning outcomes, it increases student engagement and interest in learning, and it increases the transfer of learning to another context or skill. All three combined, prepares students for the working world, whether a medical office assistant or a medical doctor.

Classroom Assessment

One component of learner-centered classrooms is "formative assessment." "Formative assessment is done while there is still time to change the outcome and it occurs prior to testing. It shapes or forms learning while it is in progress" (*Catlin, 1992*).

Classroom assessment techniques are assessment exercises done in the classroom using an informal feedback technique to gather data from students about their understanding of course content or their reactions to the instruction.

Assessment techniques assist in the application of learner-centered techniques. For example, a problem-based activity, where teams of students work collaboratively to answer questions after analyzing a case study would not be relevant without a "debrief" (large group or small team discussion) of asking students how they came to their conclusions.

The value of assessment techniques in learner-centered classes is that it provides clear methods for obtaining comprehensible feedback and evaluative measurement on student learning outcomes. After faculty identify what students need to learn, assessment helps them measure whether or not they have learned it.

Weimer (2002) notes that today, faculty almost entirely evaluate student work. In learner-centered teaching, "faculty still evaluate and grade student work, but evaluation activities that involve students are now included in the process."

Students learn how to assess their own work and participate in the evaluation

1/3 of 1/3 peer 1/3 instructor

of work done by their peers. "These self- and peer assessment activities develop skills that independent, self-regulating learners need" (*Ibid.*).

Weimer (2002) concludes that learner-centered teaching does not deny the importance of grades, but expresses concern that grades and points convey a powerful message that the only learning worth doing is learning that you get points for doing. She asks, "What of that intensely satisfying pleasure derived from and through the sheer joy of learning?"

Student Engagement

Helping students become more active in their learning is a strong criterion for learner-centered classrooms. The goal is to help students "want to learn" and to guide them through a lifelong learning process. "When teachers move to the student's side of the log to observe and to reflect upon what is happening to the students seated there, impressions and reactions occur that are different from those experienced when they maintain their seat and distance" (*Katz & Henry, 1993*).

The discovery of what and how students prefer to learn sends teachers in new directions of teaching designs and approaches. When teachers help students grasp meaning, not just facts, "the students acquire more advanced skills or abilities for questioning the world about them, searching for and attaining understanding, reflection, and self-expression, and imagining, hypothesizing, interpreting, and reality-testing their ideas and those of others."

The focus of student learning in this new century includes:
1. Basic learning principles of transforming students into active learners.
2. Individualization; the process of inquiry; the ability to inquire with other people (collaborative learning).
3. Participation, support, and education as an emotional experience (*Katz and Henry, 1988; Ornstein & Hunkins, 1998*).

Norman's (1993) research indicates that the optimal environment for learning exists when a high intensity of interaction is offered through encouraged feedback and when the faculty motivate and provide a sense of direct engagement.

Most faculty have experienced the non-interested student, the sleeping student, and the non-responsive student. In a learner-centered environment, it is almost impossible for a student to not engage with the teacher or the class. Problem-based learning activities provide faculty the opportunity to discover such engagement.

Transfer of Learning

All new learning is based on previous learning. When relevancy and experience (from previous learning) are brought to the learning environment, transfer occurs (*Bronner, 2001*).

Findings also indicate transfer is adequately reflected by learners' abilities to solve a set of transfer problems right after they have engaged in an initial learning task.

Transfer also increases when learners can apply original learning in one context to multiple contexts. For example, a learner may learn Microsoft Excel spreadsheet design in the classroom, yet transfer does not occur until the learner creates graphs and charts in the context of his or her employment or designs a budget in the context of their personal home expenses.

Just as workplace trainers have discovered how to make learning relevant and transferable to the workplace, college faculty can incorporate the same concepts so that students not only pass the test, but are also able to apply the learning to other courses or to their new careers.

The concepts of transfer have been practiced to a large extent in business and industry. Referred to as "transfer of training," companies have found it is critical for employees and managers to learn and retain new skills rapidly to stay competitive.

Much of the research regarding transfer was conducted in educational settings, but flexible, non-traditional, and innovative training departments have had the greatest opportunity to test the theories. Business training organizations have discovered that transfer strategies in the workplace go beyond the training class (*Branford, J.D., Brown, A.L., & Cocking, R.R., ed., 2002*).

Problem-based learning emerged as a successful methodology for transfer of learning. New Mexico University found that students in problem-based learning courses were less threatened by their environment and more able to pursue learning independently than those in a traditional track (*Aspy, et al, 1993*).

In a recent article in the National Education Higher Education newsletter, *Advocate*, teaching and learning specialists Harper and Levine (2002) promote problem-based learning as a method for students to learn concepts and develop critical thinking skills. Whereas workplace training methods, such as problem-based learning, is a relatively new teaching method for general education, it has been used in medical schools successfully for at least three decades (*Aspy, et al, 1993; Harper and Levine, 2002*).

Workplace training techniques for transfer of learning are in alignment with the learner-centered concepts of community colleges because it encourages collaborative environments and teachers as facilitators, not lecturers (*Harper and Levine, 2002; Jensen and Davidson, 1997*).

As in the work setting, transfer of learning takes place when the teacher becomes a coach, a mentor, and an assessor of learning.

Chapter 5. Three Classroom Models

This research for problem-based learning as a teaching methodology was conducted in Southern California at College of the Desert. California serves as an example of the diversity of careers and people that community colleges must serve to educate the 21st century workforce.

This study investigated professional development practices for community college faculty to assist them in learner-centered strategies and assessment. It evaluated the use of peer mentoring and critical reflection on teacher practice as a method for developing and influencing faculty in the use of learner-centered teaching techniques.

There is growing research and evidence that all students learn at much higher standards in learning environments that are cooperative, collaborative, and supportive (*Barr & Tagg, 1995*). The study investigated whether or not problem-based learning, a teaching and instructional method utilizing cooperative, collaborative, and supportive methods, did increase the levels of learning and student engagement.

Each participating faculty member worked with the researcher/mentor to design a problem-based learning activity to evaluate student learning in a learner-centered environment.

The quantitative and qualitative data from the students evaluates their response to 1) a teacher-centered instruction (lecture) and 2) Problem-based Learning.

Mentoring Process

In March 2004, three faculty members (one full-time and two part-time) at College of the Desert in Palm Desert, California participated in a peer-mentoring project to learn a new learner-centered teaching technique.

To conduct the experiment, each faculty member met with the mentor (the author) to design a problem-based activity around a scheduled class topic. The participating faculty then facilitated the activity in their classroom.

Three surveys were administered to the students during the process:
1. A learning style assessment.
2. A survey following a lecture class.
3. A survey following a problem-based activity.

During the peer mentoring process, over a three-month period, the mentor made herself available to the participating faculty members to discuss the theory of learner-centered classrooms, to determine appropriate topics for a problem-based learning design, to select activities or resources to support the design, and to coach the implementation of the project.

The Mentor

The mentor worked full-time at the Center for Training and Development at College of the Desert, served as elected Chair of the Faculty Development Committee for four years, and managed the Faculty Resource Center. The mentor had access to multiple resources to help with instructional design of a problem-based activity.

The mentor was also a full-time tenured faculty member who taught at the college and at a university and had extensive experience in learner-centered teaching techniques for transfer and assessment of learning, including problem-based learning.

The Faculty

The three participating faculty were from three different fields of study: theatre, psychology, and business. All three faculty volunteered to critically reflect on their teaching practice and evaluate new ways to engage students and increase transfer of learning.

The three faculty entered into a peer mentoring relationship to initially explain the project and to design a problem-based activity. The business faculty member participated in a pilot of the project, with 15 students in a Principles of Management class. The feedback on this pilot project contributed to the improvement of the research design and the final design of the surveys.

Following three-months of peer mentoring, the actual delivery of the curriculum topics by the participating faculty with two different teaching methods were implemented over a three-week timeframe.

LEConR Use ?

In week one, the students and the participating faculty completed a learning assessment tool to determine if their learning style preferences were auditory, visual, kinesthetic (tactile), or a combination of two or three.

In week two (Class 1 – Lecture), the students received instruction in a teacher-centered style (primarily lecture) and completed a survey to respond to the style of teaching and to evaluate the success of their learning goals.

In week three (Class 2 – Problem-based), the students participated in a learner-centered, problem-based activity. Following the problem-based learner-centered instruction, the students completed the same survey administered the prior week to respond to the style of teaching and to evaluate the success of their learning goals. In both week two and week three, the students were required to read their textbook and complete homework assignments.

The participating faculty were coached in the design and delivery of the problem-based activity during two or three one-on-one peer mentoring meetings along with continued electronic mail communication and occasional phone calls. The faculty were free to stop by the mentor's office at any time for coaching before a class or for resource ideas for their classes throughout the semester.

There were three to four visits per faculty member for personal advice on engaging students through learner-centered activities for both the research project and for other teaching assignments. During scheduled visits, the mentor and faculty member finalized the problem-based activity and scheduled dates for implementation.

During impromptu coaching sessions on other teaching assignments, the mentor would help the faculty member apply the learner-centered and problem-based concepts to their curriculum and work through a lesson plan that would introduce new activities. The mentor offered suggestions and resource materials, but let the faculty member come to their own conclusions of what would work in their field of expertise.

Resource materials included videos, web sites, problem solving activities, case studies, assessment techniques, teaching and learning books and articles, and instructional design and implementation suggestions. The mentor and the participating faculty member discussed student learning outcomes and objectives for the class and determined the best course design to achieve those objectives.

At the completion of the peer mentoring project, the three participating faculty, along with the researcher/mentor, met as a group to evaluate the results of their:
1. Response (positive or negative) to the peer mentoring process.
2. Response (positive or negative) to delivering a problem-based activity.
3. Conclusions on the student's response (survey results) to their teaching styles.

The participating faculty had no prior contact or discussion until this meeting. The qualitative data collected from the group interview, group discussion, and critical reflection of the surveys and experience contributed to the action science-based research to determine:
1. The potential of implementing a peer mentoring program at College of the Desert.
2. The use of problem-based learning as an effective teaching and learning techniques.
3. Next steps for faculty development toward a learning college at College of the Desert.

Twenty students participated in the *Principles of Management* (business) course; 43 students participated in the *Introduction to Psychology* course; and 42 students participated in the *Introduction to Theatre* course; for a total of 105 participating students.

Learning Styles Inventory
The study evaluated learning style preferences of both faculty and students. The researcher wanted to explore the possibility that problem-based learning might be best suited for kinesthetic learners who prefer experiential, hands-on, or demonstration. Similarly explored was the possibility that an auditory learner might prefer lecture.

All participating students took a learning styles inventory to determine if their learning preference is kinesthetic, auditory, or visual (or a combination). See Appendices B and C. The inventory was designed by internationally renowned learning expert, Colin Rose (1987, 2002), author of *Accelerated Learning for the 21st Century*.

Students self-tested as 41.4% visual; 26.3% kinesthetic; 6.1% auditory; and 26.3% were a combination of two or three styles. Experimental group by learning style can be found in Table 1.

Table 1: Experimental Groups by Learning Style

Standards of learning in this research included student involvement in their own learning, student achievement of course objectives, student application of learning to the real world, and a significant learning experience as perceived by the student.

Experimental Course Group		Learning Style				Total
		Visual	Auditory	Kinesthetic	Combination	
Theatre	Count	13	3	12	11	**39**
	% in Course Experimental Group	33.3%	7.7%	30.8%	28.2%	100.0%
Psychology	Count	24	1	7	11	**43**
	% in Course Experimental Group	55.8%	2.3%	16.3%	25.6%	100.0%
Business	Count	4	2	7	4	**17**
	% in Course Experimental Group	23.5%	11.8%	41.2%	23.5%	100.0%
Total	**Count**	**41**	**6**	**26**	**26**	**99**
	% in Course Experimental Group	41.4%	6.1%	26.3%	26.3%	100.0%

"This study also looked into the teaching method preferences of the participating faculty. Faculty preferences were determined using a self-evaluation critical reflection survey (See Appendix E) to determine level of preference to "learner-centered practices" or "teacher-centered practices."

Whether a faculty member prefers one or the other, may have some bearing on his or her willingness, comfortableness, or ability to design and facilitate learning and assessment activities, such as problem-based learning. All three participating faculty were "moderate" in their teacher-centered self-evaluation and "high" in their learner-centered self-evaluation. All three educators desired a learning-centered classroom and practiced facilitation of large group discussion and student inquiry, but they were all depending primarily on lecture.

Participating faculty were highly motivated to learn a new teaching practice. Other faculty who were known to use primarily lecture-based methods, were invited to participate in the research but declined when they realized they would have to change their teaching practice for the research. Academic freedom supports a teacher's choice in "how" he or she will deliver knowledge.

The possibility of learning styles of faculty and their preference or resistance to learner-centered or teacher-centered teaching methods was also evaluated.

The findings from this study may add light to questions that have been asked for many years in education (including workplace education):
1. Do students prefer active learning over passive learning or a combination of both?
2. Is problem-based learning a "key" to transfer of learning?
3. What is more important to the real world; tests and grades, learning and application, or both?
4. How is learning defined and measured?
5. How is the learning paradigm shifted from teacher-centered to learner-centered?

The results of this research are just one piece of the puzzle to better understand learning best practices of faculty and the learning best practices of students.

The answers are as varied as individual learners, but a few of the key findings in this study will assist decision makers and change agents who are responsible for providing the best education possible to a diverse and changing community.

The Courses

Introduction to Theatre

The first week, Theater students were informed about the experimental research project and volunteered to participate. At that time they completed a learning styles assessment and were given a short presentation on the value of understanding and applying your learning style.

The students were asked to remember their learning style(s) in order to identify them in future surveys. The faculty member of the theatre class in the second week of the research project lectured extensively on "The Relationship of the Audience and the Performance."

In the lecture class there was teacher-led group discussion and students were encouraged to ask questions. During the lecture class, the teacher did give an opportunity for some students to draw, doodle, or diagram examples of the topic on the classroom white board. Other students were encouraged to diagram in their notes. There were no small group student-discussions. At the end of the class in week one, the students were given team assignments for a problem-based activity.

Students organized into teams by self-dividing into groups of five or six students each. Each group was told that they would present to the class over the next two weeks until every group had presented. The problem-based activity was to write a playwright's perspective on the topic of a production manager dealing with chronic tardiness of actors; and communicate the message to the audience through a theatrical performance.

One person was selected as a production manager and each team had to discuss the basic concepts of stage, lights, props, set, makeup, costumes, and pre-programmed computer effects that a production manager would communicate to a stage manager in their group discussions. The students worked on their assignment as a team primarily outside of class, but they were also given fifteen to twenty minutes to work on the project during each class prior to the presentations.

Following each presentation, the faculty member facilitated a "debrief" discussion using student questions and comments as a guide for group discussion. In addition to designing and delivering a theatrical production, they informed the class of the style of the performance; realistic, non-realistic, feeling, or humoristic. The students then completed a survey at the end of the lecture class in week two and again at the end of the problem-based project in week three.

Introduction to Psychology

The faculty member of the Psychology class used the same learning styles survey process described above.

During the second week of the research project she lectured extensively on psychological experiments. The lecture class was primarily guided by teacher expertise and somewhat guided by student questions that were answered by the teacher.

In week three of the research project, the teacher gave a short summary lecture on psychological experiments and the causes of depression. She used the remaining class time for a problem-based activity. In both classes the instructor assumed that textbook reading assignments were completed by the students.

In the problem-based activity, students were divided into teams and given the following case study problem to solve: "Design a psychological experiment examining the effects of a new treatment for patients suffering from major depression"; and "as a group determines what the 'new treatment' will be, and how the experiment will be designed."

Students were asked to select one or more spokespersons for the group who would explain the experiment to the class. A list of specific questions related to the process was given to each group:

1. What is your hypothesis?
2. Which group is the control group?
3. Which group is the experimental group?
4. How will the results be measured?

As each group presented the results of their group work, the instructor added expertise advice when needed. The process for group selection was a self-select decision, based primarily on where students were sitting. The students completed a survey at the end of week two's lecture and again at the end of the problem-based activity.

Principles of Management (Business)

Again, the faculty member for the Business class used the same learning styles survey process previously described.

The second week of the research project, she lectured on "History and Current Theories on Management." Using case studies from the textbook, the teacher facilitated group discussion and encouraged questions. The topic for the problem-based activity was diversity in the workplace. After a short lecture that aligned with the required reading from the textbook, the students took a personality and communication style inventory.

The instructor, using a computer slide show presentation, instructed the students on the various characteristics of each style. The students were then divided into four groups, each group representing one of the four personality styles and given a problem-based assignment.

Each group discussed their strengths, their "stretches" or weaknesses, what they could do more of or less of, to get along with other people, and a motto or song that represented them. Each personality group presented their characteristics and group answers to the whole class.

The teams were then asked to write a one paragraph letter of appreciation from the CEO to the VP of Finance who just saved the company one million dollars through her management of a strategic budget committee. Each team was assigned to write the letter to another team of a different personality and communication style, using language and reward that would match the other team personality.

A spokesperson read the letter to the team of a different style and in return the receiving team provided feedback as to the letter's impact (according to their style).

The debrief included the need to understand diversity in employees' work and communication styles and how managers need to reward and recognize employees according to their preferences and motivations.

This followed with a group discussion of how the students could use this in their workplace. The students completed a survey at the end of week two's lecture and again at the end of the problem-based activity.

Findings

The quantitative data from the research indicated the following significants factors about a learner-centered classroom using problem-based learning versus a teacher-centered classroom using lecture:

1. Students are more likely to achieve course objectives in a problem-based class;
2. All learning styles had significant increase in learning with problem-based learning;
3. Students are more likely to be involved in their own learning in a problem-based class; and
4. Students are more likely to participate in small team discussions than large group discussions.

Based on qualitative data collected from a questionnaire and a focus group, the participating faculty were pleased at the increased level of involvement of students in a problem-based activity who are "ordinarily silent and withdrawn from any class participation" (*Theatre, 2004*).

The theatre teacher commented that she purposely restrained from jumping in to "save" the groups that were having a rough time with decision-making and concluded that the risk taking was part of what the students needed to learn.

The participating faculty observed in problem-based learning the following:

1. A high degree of enthusiasm and energy.
2. Sharing of ideas amongst the majority of participants.
3. Student-groups wanting the teacher to validate their ideas and plans.
4. Real world knowledge of some students was beneficial to their

team members.

5. Social interaction brought a component of fun, making it a pleasant learning experience.
6. Lots of discussion and working together (collaboration).
7. Looking up information in the text (critically thinking).
8. More questions were asked.
9. The classroom environment was perceived to be safer for student to participate.

The participating faculty believe that the problem-based activity made a substantial impact on the students in the following ways:

1. Faculty observed many students expressing an increased interest and respect for the subject matter.
2. The Theatre teacher observed that there was a greater degree of reflective commenting done after the peer presentations than there ever was after a lecture or video presentation.
3. The Psychology teacher appreciated the way students take a more active role than a passive role.
4. The Business teacher believes the students will definitely retain the fundamental principles to a greater degree due to the student participation in the learning.

The Business teacher did note, however, that there were details and specifics on the subject matter that would have been included in a traditional lecture that these students did not get to hear.

This comment led to the question, "is problem-based learning or other learner-centered activities worth the 'trade-off' to 'let go' of other details and specifics on the subject matter?"

The response was three-fold:

1. Students must realize that they are responsible keeping up on the reading in the textbook.
2. Many of the details are threaded throughout the rest of the course for student learning.
3. The "shelf life" of participating in an activity was going to be longer than remembering any lecture theory taught.

The consensus was "each topic needed to be assessed for suitability" for problem-based learning or other learner-centered activities and some classes would need to remain lecture and practice based (such as accounting).

For course topics considered appropriate for learning-centered activities, the consensus was that the trade off would be worth the time invested. Participating faculty affirmed that problem-based learning was enjoyable and that they would much rather facilitate the exploration of course content rather than giving them the answers.

The following was also acknowledged regarding problem-based learning:
1. The teacher must have very clear expectations as to what the student learning outcomes for the activity are.
2. The outcomes must clearly be conveyed and understood by the students (otherwise, students may enjoy the project, but fall short of learning specific content).
3. It is time consuming and most classes are too short to implement a problem-based activity.
4. Careful instructional planning must first take place.

Even given the above challenges, all participating faculty stated they would include more problem-based activities in their courses, especially earlier in the semester to encourage communication between students. They agreed that they would continue to assess the suitability of this teaching technique, depending on topic, even if just to augment many of the principles.

Participating faculty agreed that problem-based learning is only effective if the facilitator (teacher) helps the students "connect the dots" with a "debrief" of the activity at the conclusion of each presentation or case study.

It became clear early on in the project that the techniques could be appropriate in their application to a wide variety of subject matters. The Psychology teacher had extensive experience in problem-based learning, but found it helpful to get additional suggestions for the activity and adding questions that she had not considered. Having a mentor was the greatest positive aspect of the research participation.

The Business instructor noted, "This was a great fit for me. As a fairly new instructor, I loved the input from someone more experienced."

There was a consensus that in the cases where student classes were longer than two hours per session, the problem-based activities were really needed to keep interest and energy level up. It is for those classes that they all would like to continue to have access to resources and ideas.

The quantitative data from the student surveys was not intended to scientifically prove that problem-based learning is a preferred teaching technique over lecture. The intent was to evaluate whether or not there was any significant difference in learning outcomes and student learning experiences as perceived by the students.

The quantitative data helped participating faculty evaluate if it was worth the time and effort spent on designing the class activity around the course content. Rather than teaching faculty theories on learner-centered techniques, the researcher recruited faculty to participate in a problem-based design and implementation.

Results

Study teams or collaborative group activities in or out of the classroom are encouraged by the notion that "students can often do as a group what they cannot do by themselves and that students benefit from peer teaching – explanation, comments, and instruction from their course-mates" (*Davis, 2001*). There is yet another level of learning that occurs in teams. "Students must build a social environment and learn the skills of negotiation and conflict resolution necessary for democratic problem solving" (*Joyce, et al, 2000*).

In this study, it was found that students were more actively involved in their learning through the problem-based activity and received a higher level of feedback from students.

The students ranked their understanding of the course objectives in both the lecture and problem-based class as high, but there was an increase in problem-based learning. Achieving course objectives in the Theatre class increased from 72.5% to 84.6%; Psychology increased from 67.7% to 87.5%; and Business increased from 73.7% to 93.8%.

In the qualitative analysis with the faculty focus group, the faculty confirmed that they took extra care and time in explaining the course objectives prior to the problem-based activity because they did not want the learning outcome to get lost in the energy and fun of the activity. Achieving course objectives is a controversial topic when discussing learner-centered classrooms. In order to implement problem-based activities, some content may need to go. The results of the analysis of this survey question, shows that course objectives were achieved in a learner-centered environment.

Weimer (2002) notes that when she does her own course planning, she tries to focus on a related question: "What is it my students need to know and be able to do during their professional lives? What skills and knowledge will stand the test of time, given the dynamic nature of knowledge and information?"

The qualitative data from the focus group revealed that a majority of students were taking Theatre and Psychology as part of a general education degree, and were not necessarily planning on using the problem-based activity in their careers. In contrast, the Business class had a majority of students already working in the Business field and their concept of "real world" application was higher.

In future research, if nursing students and/or other vocational students participated in a similar research project, the results may be significantly higher.

When students compared the problem-based method to lecture, they found the quality of learning higher in problem-based. The Theatre class increased from 68.3% to 82.1%; Psychology increased from 90.5% to 97.1%; and Business increased from 77.8% to 81.3%.

Learning Styles

Davis (2001) notes that "there is no consensus in the research about whether matching teaching methods to learning styles increases learning; some research shows no measurable gains in matching instruction to students' learning preference."

Other research suggests that there may be relationships between culture and learning styles, but some argue against this with concern that it could reinforce stereotypes (*Davis, 2001*).

The author's hypothesis that kinesthetic learners would improve learning with problem-based learning techniques and auditory learners would improve learning with lecture techniques, was not proven. In fact, all learners of all learning styles increased in learning and student engagement with problem-based learning versus lecture.

What does work, according to Davis (2001) is to vary teaching strategies, assignments, and learning activities to meet the needs of all students. Learning style preferences may have more to do with how students prefer to conduct their own learning than how they respond to how a subject is taught.

Students usually prefer to work with students whose learning styles are similar to their own (*Davis, 2001*). But some research suggests that they will "learn less effectively because they reinforce one another's weaknesses instead of developing new strengths by working with a variety of learners."

Teachers understanding their own learning style may have an impact on understanding how they need to take more care in teaching to other learning styles.

For example, teachers who are more visual or auditory may want to take the time to develop course materials drawing on students' kinesthetic (hands on) needs. Davis (2001) encourages teachers to create a variety of classroom instruction rather than change teaching instruction to match a group of students that may primarily be one learning style.

He notes that "there is no consensus in the research about whether matching teaching methods to learning styles increases learning; some research show no measurable gains in matching instruction to students' learning preference."

Other research frequently supports that it is "how" or "to what degree" a student uses their learning style to outperform others in a given course regardless of which teaching method is used (*Davis, 2001*).

Curriculum Development

Change begins in increments in higher education, and Weimer (2002) notes that, "Perhaps as more individual faculty begins teaching this way; their collective influence on curricular development will grow."

The faculty that participated in this research agreed that for appropriate topics, problem-based learning was worth the effort of spending time on design, not just for the increased learning results, but to get students engaged and to develop a love of learning.

Fink (2003) cites three problems teachers face in learning in higher education:
1. Getting students prepared for class.
2. Avoiding student boredom.
3. Poor retention of knowledge.

He believes to improve student retention of knowledge (or increase transfer of learning) colleges have two choices: a) provide students with a refresher course during inter-session or b) redesign the course to give students more experience using what they have learned. Fink proposes that redesigning of courses will provide more application opportunities, address the classroom problems that teachers face, and will improve the quality of educational curricula.

"While I clearly understand and acknowledge the important role that content knowledge and interaction have in teaching, I have become convinced over the years that learning how to design courses is the missing link that can integrate new ideas about teaching, solve major teaching problems, and allow institutions to offer better support for faculty and better educational programs for students and for society" (*Fink, 2003*).

The faculty want to continue to understand and use problem-based learning in their courses, but they are going to need assistance with instructional design and the college's support to make this happen to any significant degree.

Organizational Support

Colleges throughout the nation are facing the challenge of change and improvement in teaching and learning. The fact remains that it is a college's teachers who will ultimately decide if this is going to happen. As faculty discover benefits of learner-centered methods through education or peer mentoring programs, they "are still not likely to make the decision to change without support from their institutions" (*Fink, 2003*). "They need to feel that their institutions truly value better learning and better teaching and are willing to provide faculty with what they need in order to learn new ways of teaching: time, encouragement, institutional centers that can provide the ideas that faculty need, reward, and so on" (*Ibid.*).

The following are recommendations for organizational support of faculty who want to learn new ways of teaching and assessment:
1. Make sure the institution is organized and operates in a way that is internally in alignment.
2. Institutional support of faculty efforts to learn about new ideas on teaching and learning by making professional development an integral part of faculty work and establishing centers that can help faculty learn new ideas about teaching and learning.
3. Have institutional leaders, especially department deans, who can work with faculty in deciding how to make time available for professional development.
4. Evaluate teaching in a way that will foster a faculty perspective on teaching that is focused on student learning and on what they need to do to further enhance the quality of their teaching.
5. Develop mechanisms for educating students about what constitutes good teaching and learning, so they can cooperate with faculty who use new ideas (*Fink, 2003*).

Teachers continually face the question of whether to keep teaching the way they always have or to learn new concepts. Research may indicate the need for better learning by students, institutions can better prove support for faculty who want to change and improve, but ultimately the paradigm shift from teacher-centered to learner-centered will not take place without faculty commitment.

CHAPTER 6. Problem-based Learning Activities

Most scenarios, simulations, role plays, or case studies are going to reflect the real world. Thus, the examples noted in this chapter are from real world training departments in Fortune 500 companies. Faculty are encouraged to design their own scenarios to reflect his or her field of study.

Case Studies

Case studies are often used in problem-based learning. The case study method originated in the teaching of law and medicine and has most often been extended to the teaching of business, including business ethics, leadership, and project management.

Students are presented with a real-life problem. "A good case study presents a realistic situation and includes the relevant background, facts, conflicts, and sequences of events – up to the point requiring a decision or action. As students analyze and discuss the case, they retrace and critique the steps taken by the key characters and try to deduce the outcome (*Davis, 2001*)."

Typically the case study is a simple descriptive scenario of employees, managers, customers, or projects that are in crisis, have an ethical dilemma, or need quality improvement. A specific set of questions is often asked to help learners generate some solutions for the "real life" situation. These types of case studies can be real stories obtained during a needs assessment of an organization, "borrowed" from other instructional designs, created by the instructor or designer to best reflect the course objectives and learners, or created by the students themselves during the facilitation of the course.

More in-depth case studies include psychological or medical symptoms that are diagnosed, company issues described in Harvard Business Review, or problems to be solved in the field of economics, environment, or human resources.

A way for students to create their own case study and develop problem-solving skills is for student to share real life challenges. Students select the "case" from the team that they want to work on. It could be a problem for a project management class, a medical issue in a nursing class, a quality control issue that a student may have at work, or a career challenge. Students apply their knowledge from the course in addition to their own personal experiences to identify a solution. Students also share how they problem-solved, how they came to a consensus, how they managed conflict in the process, and how they identified an action plan.

Facilitating problem-based learning around real challenges in the workplace is extremely effective. It gives great return on investment for the working students. If the class lacks experienced workers that other students can learn from - case studies can be found in most textbooks.

Simulations

A simulation attempts to "approximate realistic conditions so that the concepts learned and problem-solutions generated are transferable to the real world and to understanding and performing tasks related to the content of the simulation" (*Joyce, Weil, & Calhoun, 2000*).

Some simulations are games, some are competitions, and some create a business environment with tables, chairs, and supplies, such as a bank or a customer service company. Technical simulations are often in manufacturing sites to prepare people for the real assembly line or for safety practices. Students in a medical billing class can simulate doing billing on a software program. All the simulations give students an opportunity to practice, problem-solve, and find solutions through an individual or team process when problems are encountered.

Corporate Examples of Problem-Based Learning

Hewlett-Packard Ink Jet Printer Division, Vancouver, WA

Hewlett-Packard training departments have often used the "Starship Simulation" as a problem-based learning activity to encourage total quality control – process improvement. A simulated classroom environment is set up to reflect a manufacturing site of paper starships. Each table is a "department" of the company. There are "painters," "cutters," "supply," "assembly 1," "assembly 2," and "quality control."

The problems, purposely built into the game simulation, include: a shortage of supplies, a required paper trail for supplies, defective painting tools, dull scissors, vague directions, no training, and an incompetent, uninformed supervisor. In addition, the rules and processes that are enforced by the facilitator are non-empowering, lower morale, and limit productivity.

Following 30 minutes of poor production and Starships that fail quality control, the learners are asked to identify what the problems were. Using a problem-solving tool, called the Fishbone Diagram, learners identify major categories of tools, people, resources, equipment, and policy and then list specific problems in each area. They then prioritize their problem identification through a multi-voting system and determine the top five problems they will address. Each team takes one of the problems, brainstorms solutions and writes an action plan.

At the end of the training, the learners reflect on a real problem in their department and write an action plan to propose to their supervisor. The intent and outcome of this instructional design is to teach employees to problem solve, process improve, communicate with supervisors, and take responsibility for the success of the organization.

Mechanical Engineering and Biomedical Engineering, Technische University, Canada

Problem-based learning has been implemented as a partial strategy for Mechanical Engineering and Biomedical Engineering at Technische University in Canada. In its original form, the problem-based curriculum is delivered as a set of problems that provides the starting point for the learning process and is the backbone of the curriculum.

Students first encounter problems, instead of facts and theories. Professional reasoning skills are developed and learning needs are identified in a cooperative setting with a tutor. Next is the individual self-directed study, motivated by the previous stage in the cycle. The cycle is closed by a co-operative phase again: applying newly gained knowledge to the problem and summarizing what has been learned. The next cycle starts with a new problem. "Although lecturing seems to be an easy and efficient way of just giving students the knowledge they need, it does not take into account students' ability to absorb that information and its later usefulness. There is also little concern [in lecture] for the students' ability to reason or their self-learning skills (*Perrenet, 2000*)."

In this university class, students use their real world experiences first to encounter a problem. Second, they learn the facts and theories and encounter the problem with a different perspective. This process opens students minds to new concepts and problem-solving methods.

South Carolina Advanced Technological Education Center of Excellence

The South Carolina Advanced Technological Education Center of Excellence is teaching students through an innovative approach that brings relevance to the learning process by simulating a real world, high-tech workplace. "The center uses an integrated, problem-based curriculum, collaborative teaching strategies and extensive active-learning techniques that are implemented through faculty and student teamwork (*Reese, 2001*)."

For example, instead of learning an area of math that will be used months later when they are studying physics, both are explored at the same time. Students start with a problem, learn the math, science and communications necessary to solve the problem, then arrive at the solution by working in teams. Problems are sometimes open ended, so different teams come up with different solutions (as in the real world).

"With more than 15,000 technology-based jobs to be filled in South Carolina – and a projected continuing growth of technology jobs – this initiative has drawn attention and praise from the business and industrial community in the state, including Honda, Roche Carolina, Robert Bosch Corporation and Michelin (*Reese, 2001*)." The Honda Manager of Administration, Jeffrey Helton says, "The ATE program is right in line with what industry needs today."

The College Classroom

Learner-centered concepts are not meant to challenge a professor's expertise. Getting a great academic education is not in question. What is in question is: will the student be able to critically think and will the student be prepared to succeed in the working world?

Medical universities decided that intensive internships with practical application increased learning. Technology companies discovered that engineers thrown into a project immediately out of college was more effective than giving new employees more company-specific "classroom education." The Saturn car company became successful by letting the employees make decisions, solve problems, and choose their own training.

In the college classroom, problem-based learning can be as simple as letting students brainstorm a list rather than presenting a list; or working on a math problem in a group setting. It can also be integrating project management software training with lessons of leadership, business writing, and time management. The more integration of skills, the more likely the retention of knowledge and transfer of skills to the workplace.

One teacher from Florida testified at an International Teaching and Learning Conference that he knew learning was taking place when he removed himself from the head of the classroom and leaned against the wall. When he was leaning against the wall, he was observing the students practicing the theories. With excitement, he was watching students learn how to learn.

Donald L. Finkel and G. Stephen Monk are professors at The Evergreen State College, Olympia, Washington. They have used learning groups and problem-based learning for the past 15 years and have worked systematically with teachers from diverse disciplines to change their teaching style.

They note that "a teacher who takes responsibility for all that goes on in the class gives students no room to experiment with ideas, to deepen their understanding of concepts, or to integrate concepts into a coherent system" (*Finkel & Monk, 1983*).

In problem-based learning, the role of the teacher changes from expert to helper. Finkel and Monk propose that teachers will have to distinguish between teaching and learning roles and "functions." Roles imply the duty and responsibility of the teacher and of the student. Function implies who or what can best serve the student to assist transfer of learning. In problem-based learning, students can access available resources and methods to solve the problem or case study put before them. It truly becomes a learning journey, where more is gained from the process than from the final outcome.

Chapter 7. Call to Action

The theories of learning styles, multiple intelligences, collaborative learning, experiential learning, or problem-based learning have grabbed the attention of many educators around the country.

The unfortunate news is there are thousands of schools and colleges who are still teaching through dry lectures, boring worksheets, and large textbooks. Problem-based learning touches every learning style and several multiple intelligences during one class session.

Problem-based learning brings a wealth of enrichment to any field of study. The benefits (listed in Table 2) range from "diversity appreciation," to "critical thinking development, to "relevance to the real world." At the same time it is an opportunity to make theory and textbook learning more relevant.

There are over 75 student learning outcomes that can be accomplished in just one well-planned problem-based activity (see Appendix G). Major outcomes include:

1. Thinking skills
2. Research skills
3. Resource locating skills
4. Writing skills
5. Display-making skills
6. Group-work skills
7. Speaking skills
8. Self-assessment skills

Workplace skills, referred to as "secondary skills" or "integrated skills" include:

1. Consensus decision-making.
2. Diversity appreciation.
3. Teamwork.
4. Time management.
5. Planning and organizing.
6. Crisis management.
7. Goal setting.
8. Flexibility.

9. Interpersonal communications.
10. Conflict resolution.
11. Risk taking.
12. Critical thinking.
13. Transfer of learning to real world application.

Table 2: Problem-based Learning Benefits

	Helps instructors know that the student got it.
	Works well with all diverse learners (diversity appreciation).
	Encourages students to learn how to learn together.
	Allows students to be the active focus for learning.
	Requires shared responsibility for learning.
	Promotes critical thinking and intellectual discovery.
	Creates an instructional strategy that aligns with student learning outcomes.
	Provides an opportunity for assessment.
	Creates an opportunity for the teachers to serve as expert mentors and coaches.
	Focuses on process in addition to content.
	Brings out the learners' belief system for examination and testing.
	Makes room for all ideas through open communication, consensus decision making.
	Provides opportunity to learn from mistakes.
	Gives immediate relevance to the real world.
	Promotes a problem-centered and learner-centered approach to learning.
	Allows for feedback from students and the instructor.
	Increases transfer of learning.
	Decreases knowledge decay.
	Integrates learning contexts.
	Integrates secondary workplace objectives (flexibility, teamwork, decision making)
	Allows the learner to use existing knowledge and apply it.
	Influences the cognitive process.
	Prepares students for the working world.
	Uses Blooms Taxonomy.

Problem-based learning moves students from "Knowledge" on the Bloom's Taxonomy Chart to "Analysis" and "Synthesis" (See Appendix H). In my Principles of Management class, I require students to interview a manager in the real world and ask questions about the leaders influencing skills, planning and organizing skills, controlling skills, and problem-solving skills. They ask the manager about their greatest challenges and what they would do differently regarding their education and career path.

In this simple assignment, students are able to identify, interpret, and conclude what management is explaining (See Appendix F). When students come to class they meet in teams, compare and contrast, evaluate, and analyze their results. Students find a common thread of challenges and successes in real world management. Many earn a new respect for their boss. Others realize their personal leadership gaps and assess additional training needs. Most are finally able to connect the dots between the textbook and the real world.

Some students stated that what they learned in that one problem-based activity of inquiry, research, and discussion exceeded everything else they learned about management. The theory of management became something and someone real to them.

Rigorous Classrooms and Effective Teachers

The author does not promote an "easy" classroom of "fun activities." Problem-based activities need to be well planned, challenging, and rigorous. The more challenging the case study or problem – the higher level of critical thinking.

At a North Central Regional Educational Laboratory, educational strategies for student success were researched. The following was hilighted:

1. Intensifying learning helps build high-achieving schools, which in turn are most likely to produce successful, high-achieving students. High-achieving schools are rigorous schools. They develop rigorous standards, a rich curriculum, knowledgeable and skilled teachers, and meaningful learning experiences as essential elements (*Wheelock, 1998*).

69

2. Effective teachers "know the content they are teaching, engage students in learning, and challenge them to greater accomplishments" (U.S. Department of Education, 1999).

3. Skilled teachers intensify learning by providing meaningful assignments while holding high expectations for all students. Such assignments deal with the significant concepts of a discipline, incorporate higher-order thinking skills, are connected to the "real world," and allow substantial time for discussion and idea sharing among students.

4. In these environments, students work together to frame their own questions and investigate them. Active environments require collaboration and communication, and encourage more analysis, synthesis, and evaluation of information than do traditional classrooms (North Central Regional Educational Laboratory, 2000).

5. Active learning environments require students to take responsibility for their own learning and develop strategies for learning (*Costello, 1996*). Instruction in active environments emphasizes depth of learning rather than breadth of learning (*Peterson, 1995*).

6. Teachers and researchers participating in a longitudinal research study conducted by Apple Computer, Inc. found that high levels of student involvement in learning occurred most often in classrooms that encouraged active learning. In the Apple Classrooms of Tomorrow, students were encouraged to frame their own questions and were urged to follow up on them. The students frequently worked in groups, and the atmosphere was a collaborative one—among students as well as between students and teachers (North Central Regional Educational Laboratory, 2000).

Active learning environments – learner-centered classrooms – lead to student success, student retention, and student preparation for the 21st Century working world.

References

ACCJC Standards, Adopted 2002. Accrediting Commission for Community and Junior Colleges Western Association of Schools and Colleges, 1–28.

Angelo, T. A., & Cross, K. P. (1993). *Classroom Assessment Techniques: A Handbook for College Teachers* (2nd ed.). San Francisco, CA: Jossey-Bass.

Argyris, C. *Action science and organizational learning.* Journal of Managerial Psychology, Bradford, 1995, pages 1–9.

Argyris, C. *The next challenge for TQM – taking the offensive on defensive reasoning.* The Journal for Quality and Participation, Nov/Dec 1999, Volume 22, Issue 6.

Argyris, C., & Schon, D. (1996) *Organizational learning II: Theory, Method, and Practice.* Reading, MA: Addison-Wesley Longman.

Aspy, D.N., Aspy C.B., & Quinby, P.M. *What Doctors Can Teach Teachers about Problem-Based Learning. Educational Leadership,* April 1993, pages 22–24.

Ast, John Van. *Community College Faculty: Making the Paradigm Shift.* Community College Journal of Research & Practice, September 1999, Volume 23, Issue 6.

Balch, D (2002). *Curriculum Foundation for Course Design.* Instructor Presentation for ED7711 Course Design. Capella University (2002).

Barr, R.B., & Tagg, J. *From Teaching to Learning – A New Paradigm for Undergraduate Education,* Change, Nov/Dec 95, Volume 27, Issue 6.

Branford, J.D., Brown, A.L., & Cocking, R.R., ed. (2002). *How People Learn.* Retrieved February 3, 2002 from http://books.nap.edu/html/howpeople1.

Bridges, D. (2000). *Back to the Future: the higher education curriculum in the 21st century.* Cambridge Journal of Education, 30(1), 37-53.

Brown, D.M. (2003). *Learner-Centered Conditions That Ensure Students' Success in Learning.* Education, Fall 2003, Volume 124, Issue 1.

Brown, K.L. (2003). *From Teacher-Centered to Learner-centered Curriculum: Improving Learning in Diverse Classrooms.* Education, Fall 2003, Volume 124, Issue 1.

Bush, G.W. (2004) FACT SHEET: JOBS FOR THE 21st CENTURY. Sherzer Press Releases, Wednesday, January 21, 2004. Perrysburg Township, Ohio: THE WHITE HOUSE Office of the Press Secretary.

California Community Colleges (1996). *Faculty Participation in Accreditation* (ED 395 629). Sacramento, CA: Academic Senate.

Cascadia Community College. (2001). *Cascadia's Learning Experience.* Retrieved January 12, 2002 http://www.cascadia.ctc.edu/teaching_and_learning/learning_experience.htm

Chall, J.S. (2000). *The academic achievement challenge: What really works in the classroom?* New York: Guildford.

Cross, K. P. (1981). *Adults as Learners.* San Francisco: Jossey-Bass, Inc.

Cross, K. P. *Leading-Edge Efforts to Improve Teaching and Learning.* The Hesburg Awards. Change, July/August 2001, Volume 33, Issue 4.

Cross, K.P., & Angelo, T.A. (1988). *Classroom Assessment Techniques: A Handbook for Faculty.* Ann Arbor, Michigan: National Center for Research to Improve Postsecondary Teaching and Learning.

Davis, B. G. (2001). *Tools for Teaching.* San Francisco, CA: Jossey-Bass.

Delpit, L. (1995). *Other people's children: Cultural conflict in the classroom.* New York: New Press.

Denton, Janice (2003). *Teacher as Grader, Teacher as Assessor: Changing Roles?* Assessment Presentation given at College of the Desert, April 2003.

Drummond, T. (2002). A Brief Summary of the Best Practices in Teaching. Retrieved on July 1, 2003 from: http://northonline.sccd.ctc.edu/eceprog/bstpract.html

Fink, L.D. (2003). *Creating Significant Learning Experiences: An Integrated Approach to Designing College Courses.* San Francisco: John Wiley & Son.

Finkel, D., & Monk, G. S. (1983). *Teachers and Learning Groups. Case Studies - Changing the Teacher's Role.* Retrieved April 18, 2002 from http://www.biochem.wisc.edu/attie/articles/Atlas_Complex.pdf

Forman, D.C. (2002). *Training Highly Skilled Audiences.* Performance Xpress, October 2002, www.performanceexpress.org/mainframe0211.html

Gates, R. & Cooksey, R.W (1998). *Learning to manage and managing to learn.* Journal of Workplace Learning, Volume 10, Issue 1.

George, D. *Faculty Development Committee Report.* College of the Desert, May 2000.

Halpern, D. F., & Associates (1994). *Changing College Classrooms: New Teaching and Learning Strategies for an Increasingly Complex World.* San Francisco, CA: Jossey-Bass.

Harnish, D. & Wild, L.A. *Mentoring Strategies for Faculty Development.* Studies in Higher Education, 1994, Volume 19, Issue 2, p191, 11p (AN 9411151780).

Harper, M. and Levine, A. *Problem-Based Learning: Engaging students actively in meaningful learning.* Advocate, NEA Higher Education, December 2002, (20)2, pages 5–8.

Henson, K.T. (2003). Foundations for Learner-Centered Education: A Knowledge Base. Education, Fall 2003, Vol. 124, Issue 1.

Jensen, E. and Davidson, N. *12-Step Recovery Program for Lectureholics.* College Teaching. Summer 1997, Volume 45, Issue 3, pages 102–103. Retrieved May 20, 2002 from http://libsys.uah.edu:2093/fulltext.asp

Joyce, B., Weil, M.,, & Calhoun, E. (2000). *Models of Teaching* (6th ed.). Needham Heights, MA: Allyn & Bacon.

Katz, J., & Henry, M. (1993). *Turning Professors Into Teachers: A New Approach to Faculty Development and Student Learning* (2nd ed.). Phoenix, AZ: The Oryx.

Knowles, M. S. (1980). *The Modern Practice of Adult Education: From Pedagogy to Andragogy* (2nd ed.). New York: Cambridge Books.

Kolb, D. A. (1984). *Experiential Learning: Experience as The Source of Learning and Development.* Englewood Cliffs, NJ: Prentice Hall.

Law, B. (1994). Hiring the Right Next Generation of Faculty. *Leadership Abstracts,* volume7 n2 (Feb 1994), 1–4.

Lucey, C.A. Civic Engagement, Shared Governance, and Community Colleges. *Academe*, July 2002, Vol. 88, Issue 4.

Luna, G., & Cullen, D. L. (1995). *Empowering the Faculty: Mentoring Redirected and Renewed* (ED 399 888). Washington, DC: George Washington University.

McDonald, J.P. (2003). *Teachers studying student work: Why and how?* Phi Delta Kappan, 84 (2) 121–127.

Menges, R. J., Weimer M., and Associates (1996). *Teaching on Solid Ground: Using Scholarship to Improve Practice.* San Francisco: Jossey-Bass.

Mennin, S., Gordan, P., Majoor, G, Osman, H., & Hafiz, A.S. (2003) *Change in Learning & Practice*, Mar2003, Volume 16 Issue 1, pages 98–114 (AN 9429142).

Merriam, S. B., & Caffarella, R. S. (1991). *Learning in Adulthood.* San Francisco: Jossey-Bass.

Meyer, N. (2003) *Comprehensive Community College Overview* (Capella Course, Unit I), pages 9–39.

Mila, C. & Sanmarti, N. *A Model for Fostering the Transfer of Learning in Environmental Education.* Environmental Education Research, August 1999, 5(3), pages 237–267.

Morante, E.A., Ed.D. (2003) *A Handbook on Assessment for Two Year Colleges.* Sacramento, CA: California Community College Chancellor's Office Fund for Instructional Improvement Grant Program.

National Institute of Education (1989). *Involvement in Learning: Realizing the potential of American Higher Education.* Washington, D.C.: U.S. Department of Education.

Norman, C. (2003). *Teacher-Centered VS Learner-Centered: Exploring Appropriate Teaching Paradigms for Adult English Language Learners.* Dissertation submitted to The Claremont Graduate University and San Diego State University.

Norman, D. (1993). *Things that Make us Smart: Defending the Human Attributes in the Age of the Machine.* Addison-Wesley.

North Central Regional Educational Laboratory. (2000). *Indicator: Engaging learning environments.* Available online: http://www.ncrel.org/engauge/framewk/efp/environ/efpenvin.htm

O'Banion, T. (1997). *A Learning College for the 21st Century.* Phoenix, AZ: American Association of Community Colleges: ORYX.

Office of Educational Research and Improvement (ED) (January 1, 1996). *Acquiring Self-Knowledge for Career Development* (ERIC Digest Number 175 EDDD00036). Washington, D.C.: Eric Digests/Career Education.

Olivero, G., Bane, K, et al. *Executive Coaching as a Transfer of Training Tool: Effects on Productivity in a Public Agency. Public Personnel Management,* Winter 1997, Volume 26, Issue 4, pages 461–470.

Ornstein, A. C., & Hunkins, F. P. (1998). *Curriculum: Foundations, Principles, and Issues* (3rd ed.). Needham Heights, MA.

Perrenet, J. C. (2000). *The Suitability of Problem-based Learning for Engineering Education: Theory and Practice.* Teaching in Higher Education, 5(3), 345.

Peterson, K. (1995). *Creating high-achieving learning environments. Pathways to School Improvement.* Available online:
http://www.ncrel.org/sdrs/areas/issues/educatrs/leadrshp/le400.htm

Posner, G. J., & Rudnitsky, A. H. (2001). *Course Design: A Guide to Curriculum Development for Teachers* (6th ed.). New York: Addison Wesley Longman.

Reyes, M. (1992). *Challenging venerable assumptions: Literacy instruction for linguistically different students.* Harvard Educational Review, 62 (4), 427–446.

Richart, V.M. (2001) Virtual Center for Community College Transformation. Retrieved January 13, 2002 from
http://www.cascadia.ctc.edu/Transformation/consideration/change-1.htm

Rowley, J. (1998). Creating a learning organization in higher education. *Industrial and Commercial Training,* Vol. 30, No. 1, pp. 16–18.

Savoie, J.M., & Hughes, A.S. *Problem-based Learning as a Classroom Solution.* Educational Leadership 52, Number 3 (November 1994) (EJ492 914).

Senge, P., Roberts, C., Ross, R., Smith, B., & Kleiner, A. (1994). *The Fifth Discipline Fieldbook: Strategies and Tools for Building a Learning Organization.* New York: Doubleday.

Silverman, S. L., & Casazza, M. E. (2000). *Learning & Development: Making Connections to Enhance Teaching.* San Francisco: Jossey-Bass.

Smerdon, B. & Burkam, D.T. (1999). *Access to constructivist and didactic teaching: Who gets it? Where is it practiced?* Teachers College Record, 101 (1), 5–35.

Smith, C. & Cruz J. G. (1993). Guidelines for the Implementation of the Flexible Calendar Program: Academic Senate for California Community Colleges and in cooperation with the Chancellor's Office Program Staff, adopted April 3, 1883.

Smith, C., DeVol M., & Stetson, N. (2003). *Evaluating Staff and Organizational Development.* California Community College Council for Staff Development and Community College League of California, 1993, Revised 2000: Sacramento, CA.

Thernstrom, A. and Thernstrom, S. (2003). *No Excuses: Closing the Racial Gap in Learning.* New York: Simon & Schuester.

U.S. Department of Education. (1999, May). *Taking responsibility for ending social promotion: A guide for educators and state and local officials.* Available online:
http://www.ed.gov/pubs/socialpromotion/index.html

Vaughn, G.B. (2000) *The Community College Story* (2nd edition). Washington D.C.: The American Association of Community Colleges.

Vella, J. and Associates (2004). *Dialogue Education at Work: A Case Book.* San Francisco: Jossey-Bass.

Weimer, M. (2002). *Learner-centered Teaching.* San Francisco: John Wiley.

Wheelock, A. (1998). *Extra help and support to meet standards and prevent grade retention.* Available online:
http://wwwcsteep.bc.edu/ctestweb/retention/retention2.html

Appendix A
Glossary

Assessment
The systematic collection of data and information across courses, programs and the institution with a focus on outcomes, especially student learning outcomes, but also includes process, especially in seeking ongoing improvement.

In class this requires students to perform as task rather than take a test in a real-life context or a context that simulates a real-life context. Designed to judge students' abilities to use specific knowledge and skills and actively demonstrate what they know rather than recognize or recall answers to questions.

Other examples of assessment of actual student learning, competency or performance can include essays, speeches, recitals, capstone experiences and portfolios. (*Morante, 2003*).

Classroom Assessment
The process of using informal feedback techniques in which data is systematically gathered from students frequently and anonymously about their understanding of course content and reactions to instruction.

Classroom assessment could also include questions about student attitudes and background which may contribute to or impede their learning, (*Catlin, et al, 1992*).

Classroom assessment activities are conducted by an individual teacher in his or her class. The teacher chooses the assessment instrument, evaluates the data, and uses that data to determine what can be done to better student learning.

Examples of classroom assessment include quizzes, tests, Classroom Assessment Techniques (CATs), and Primary Trait Analysis (PTA).

Critical Reflection
Critical reflection involves a self-evaluation process that could lead to discovering weaknesses in what teachers do in order for meaningful change and improvement to take place. It can include collaborative conversation and brainstorm sessions involving colleagues and in a positive way, to move instructors into forthcoming changes without feeling threatened. (*Silverman and Casazza, 2000, p. 237*).

Faculty Development
Faculty development is a process that seeks to promote professional and individual

75

growth and development of college personnel, directly or indirectly involved with students.

California Community Colleges can use one to fifteen days of the state-mandated 175-day teaching year for faculty development. (*Smith & Cruz, 1993; Smith, et al, 2003*).

Learning College

A learning college is an environment where people can make decisions and formulate instructional strategies to create a learner-centered institution.

In community colleges, the goal is learning success, student performance, and increasing the ability to manage change.

"Long committed to teaching as a strategy to help students make passionate connections to learning, the community college is strategically positioned to lead the way in creating a learning college for the twenty-first century" (*O'Banion, 1997, p. 101*).

Learning Organization

A learning organization is skilled at creating, acquiring, and transferring knowledge, and at modifying its behavior to reflect new knowledge and insights. An organization where people continually expand their capacity to create the results they truly desire, where new and expansive patterns of thinking are nurtured, where collective aspiration is set free, and where people are continually learning how to learn together (*Senge, 1996*).

Learner-centered Environment or Classroom

The learner-centered environment is an approach to learning where teachers believe that the differences in students' styles of learning, experiences, and life circumstances are significant enough to make a major impact on what students need to learn, the pace at which they need to learn it, and the support they need from teachers and others to learn it (*Brown, 2003*).

Teachers bring command and expertise of content knowledge but design flexibility for learners to construct their learning. "Learner needs and characteristics take precedence over knowledge of facts and skills; the emphasis is on engaging learners in learning for understanding and thinking, to help them build their own interpretations" (*p. 3*).

Mentoring

A mentoring relationship is one in which more experienced professors guide, facilitate, and transfer knowledge to graduate students, or junior faculty.

Peer Mentoring
Peer mentoring, also referred to as "mutual mentoring," is a faculty relationship where faculty members, equal in experience or not, guide and transfer knowledge to each other usually in an instructional improvement strategy.

Unlike conventional mentoring relationships, there are not always significant differences in age, experience, rank or hierarchical levels in mentor projects.

Participants achieve a level of mutual expertise, frequently absent from traditional mentoring relationships (*Harnish & Wild, 1994*).

Problem-based Learning (PBL)
Problem-based Learning is a method of learning in which students first encounter a problem, followed by a student-centered inquiry process. Both content and the process of learning are emphasized.

Typically five to eight students work collaboratively in a group. Active discussion and analysis of problems and learning issues among students are essential to the process, enabling students to acquire and apply content knowledge and to learn and practice both individual and group communication skills critical to learning and teachings.

Problems, sometimes referred to as cases or case studies, are created/selected by the faculty that simulate professional practice or a real life situation (*Mennin, et al, 2003*).

Professional Development
Professional development educational are activities that add knowledge and skills to an individual's discipline, career, or vocation intended to improve performance on the job.

Rubric
A rubric is a set of scoring guidelines for evaluating students' work. Typically a rubric will consist of a scale used to score students' work on a continuum of quality.

Descriptors provide standards or criteria for judging the work and assigning it to a particular place on the continuum.

Rubrics make explicit the standards by which a student's work is to be judged and the criteria on which that judgment is based (*Morante, 2003*).

Student Learning Outcomes
Student learning outcomes are the competencies and skills expected of students as

they complete a course, program or institution (*Morante, 2003*).

When statements of intended outcomes are written in terms of what the students will be able to do, know or think and include some rough approximation of criteria for program success, then the minimum conditions for an acceptable outcome statement have probably been met (*Denton, 2003*).

Teacher-centered Environment or Classroom

The teacher-centered environment involves a teacher bringing their expertise into the learning context. Traditionally, teachers decide what students should learn and how.

Student interaction is basically responding to teacher-directed questions and achievement is measured on objective tests.

There is very little time for teachers in this environment to pose open-ended questions or to work on problem-based projects (*McDonald, 2003*).

Teaching Methods

Teaching methods are strategies for presentation and facilitation of learner interaction.

Transfer of Learning

Transfer of learning takes place when existing knowledge, abilities and skills assist learners in the performance of new tasks or affect the next step in the learning process.

Often, what is learned in the classroom is not transferred until the student successfully applies or practices the learning in a new or work situation.

In summary, transfer of learning occurs when the learning in one context or with one set of materials impacts the performance in another context or with other related materials (*Mila and Sanmarti, 1999*).

Appendix B
Learning Styles

Note: Used as a handout for students after participating in learning styles assessment. (Source Unknown)

Introduction to Learning Styles

Are you having trouble learning new information in your class? You may want to learn more about your unique learning style. Your learning style is the way you prefer to learn. It doesn't have anything to do with how intelligent you are or what skills you have learned. It has to do with how your brain works most efficiently to learn new information. Your learning style has been with you since you were born.

There's no such thing as a "good" learning style or a "bad" learning style. Success comes with many different learning styles. There is no "right" approach to learning. We all have our own particular way of learning new information. The important thing is to be aware of the nature of your learning style. If you are aware of how your brain best learns, you have a better chance of studying in a way that will pay off when it's time to take that dreaded exam.

Visual, Auditory, or Tactile/ Kinesthetic Learner.

To get you started thinking about your learning style, think about the way in which you remember a phone number. Do you see, in your mind's eye, how the numbers look on the phone? Or can you "see" the number on that piece of paper, picturing it exactly as you wrote it down? You might be a Visual Learner. Or, perhaps you can "hear" the number in the way that someone recited it to you. In this case, you might be an Auditory Learner. If you "let your fingers do the walking" on the phone, i.e. your fingers dial the number without looking at the phone, you may be a Tactile/ Kinesthetic Learner.

This way of looking at learning style uses the different channels of perception (seeing, hearing, touching/moving) as its model. This is a somewhat simplistic view of a very complicated subject (the human brain). However, looking at learning style from a perceptual point of view is a useful place to begin.

Match Your Learning Style and Strategies

While there is no "good" or "bad" learning style, there can be a good or bad match between the way you best learn and the way a particular course is taught. Suppose you are a Visual Learner enrolled in a traditional lecture course. You feel that the instructor drones on for hours and you can't pay attention or stay interested in the class. There's a mismatch here between your learning style and the instructional environment of the class. As soon as you understand this mismatch, you can find ways to adapt your style to ensure your success in the class. You might start tape recording the lectures so that you don't have to worry about missing important information. You might decide to draw diagrams that illustrate the ideas being presented in lecture. You might go to the Media Center and check out a video to help provide some additional information on course material you're not sure about. What you're doing is developing learning strategies that work for you because they are based on your knowledge of your own learning style.

The Visual/ Verbal Learning Style
You learn best when information is presented visually and in a written language format. In a classroom setting, you benefit from instructors who use the blackboard (or overhead projector) to list the essential points of a lecture, or who provide you with an outline to follow along with during lecture. You benefit from information obtained from textbooks and class notes. You tend to like to study by yourself in a quiet room. You often see information "in your mind's eye" when you are trying to remember something.

Words from the Visual/Verbal Learner: "When I study, I need a perfectly quiet room. All I want to do is spread out my books and notes and note cards on a big table and methodically go through my study materials until I have the subject matter down. I don't want any background music on. I can't stand studying with a partner. I don't want to talk about what I'm learning; I just want to read and write about it. I'm a Visual/Verbal learner. It seems that I learn best when my brain is inundated with written words. When studying, I like using gel pens and highlighters in six or seven different colors to write information on flashcards. Often, during an exam, I can remember the color of the information I'm trying to recall, and then the color memory triggers the memory of the answer I'm looking for."

Learning Strategies for the Visual/ Verbal Learner:
To aid recall, make use of "color coding" when studying new information in your textbook or notes. Using highlighter pens, highlight different kinds of information in contrasting colors.

Write out sentences and phrases that summarize key information obtained from your textbook and lecture.

Make flashcards of vocabulary words and concepts that need to be memorized. Use highlighter pens to emphasize key points on the cards. Limit the amount of information per card so your mind can take a mental "picture" of the information.

When learning information presented in diagrams or illustrations, write out explanations for the information.

When learning mathematical or technical information, write out in sentences and key phrases your understanding of the material. When a problem involves a sequence of steps, write out in detail how to do each step.

Make use of computer word processing. Copy key information from your notes and textbook into a computer. Use the print-outs for visual review.

Before an exam, make yourself visual reminders of information that must be memorized. Make "stick it" notes containing key words and concepts and place them in highly visible places —on your mirror, notebook, car dashboard, etc..

The Visual/ Nonverbal Learning Style
You learn best when information is presented visually and in a picture or design format. In a classroom setting, you benefit from instructors who use visual aids such as film, video, maps and charts. You benefit from information obtained from the pictures and diagrams in textbooks. You tend to like to work in a quiet room and may not like to work in study groups. When trying to remember something, you can often visualize a picture of it in your mind. You may have an artistic side that enjoys activities having to do with visual art and design.

Words from the Visual/Nonverbal Learner: "I have this kitchen utensil drawer at home, and it's packed full of utensils of one kind or the other. I've never been able to figure out why my husband can never find what he's looking for when he opens the drawer. He just rummages around in the drawer and looks distressed because he can't get his hands on the spatula he's looking for. Then I walk over, take one look at the drawer, and pick out the spatula quickly and easily. I realized, after taking the Learning Style Survey, that our different experiences have to do with our differing learning styles. I'm a Visual/Nonverbal Learner. I can scan a dense visual field (like my kitchen drawer) and quickly pick out an essential visual design (like the outline of the spatula). My husband, on the other hand, is a Tactile/Kinesthetic Learner. He's not going to find that spatula until he gets his hands on it— which is no small feat in a drawer as crammed full of things as our utensil drawer."

Learning Strategies for the Visual/ Nonverbal Learner:
Make flashcards of key information that needs to be memorized. Draw symbols and pictures on the cards to facilitate recall. Use highlighter pens to highlight key words and pictures on the flashcards. Limit the amount of information per card, so your mind can take a mental 'picture' of the information.

Mark up the margins of your textbook with key words, symbols, and diagrams that help you remember the text. Use highlighter pens of contrasting colors to "color code" the information.

When learning mathematical or technical information, make charts to organize the information. When a mathematical problem involves a sequence of steps, draw a series of boxes, each containing the appropriate bit of information in sequence.

Use large square graph paper to assist in creating charts and diagrams that illustrate key concepts.

Use the computer to assist in organizing material that needs to be memorized. Using word processing, create tables and charts with graphics that help you to understand and retain course material. Use spreadsheet and database software to further organize material that needs to be learned.

As much as possible, translate words and ideas into symbols, pictures, and diagrams.

The Tactile/Kinesthetic Learning Style

You learn best when physically engaged in a "hands on" activity. In the classroom, you benefit from a lab setting where you can manipulate materials to learn new information. You learn best when you can be physically active in the learning environment. You benefit from instructors who encourage in-class demonstrations, "hands on" student learning experiences, and field work outside the classroom.

Words from the Tactile/Kinesthetic Learner:

"When I was little, I could never sit for long periods of time in school, the way the other kids seemed to be able to. I just needed to move my body. I could never understand why we just sat at our desks, looked at the teacher and listened. I wondered why we never seemed to DO anything. I figured I was just a troublemaker, a bad student, and lazy. But now I see it in terms of learning style. I am a Tactile/Kinesthetic learner. I really need to be actively and physically involved when I'm learning, or nothing sinks in. This is a real challenge in college, especially in traditional lecture classes. But I take notes, and I also draw pictures all over my notebook pages—anything to keep my hands busy during lecture. Somehow this helps me stay focused on what the instructor is saying."

Strategies for the Tactile/ Kinesthetic Learner:

To help you stay focused on class lecture, sit near the front of the room and take notes throughout the class period. Don't worry about correct spelling or writing in complete sentences. Jot down key words and draw pictures or make charts to help you remember the information you are hearing.

When studying, walk back and forth with textbook, notes, or flashcards in hand and read the information out loud.

Think of ways to make your learning tangible, i.e. something you can put your hands on. For example, make a model that illustrates a key concept. Spend extra time in a lab setting to learn an important procedure. Spend time in the field (e.g. a museum, historical site, or job site) to gain first-hand experience of your subject matter.

To learn a sequence of steps, make 3'x 5' flashcards for each step. Arrange the cards on a table top to represent the correct sequence. Put words, symbols, or pictures on your flashcards — anything that helps you remember the information. Use highlighter pens in contrasting colors to emphasize important points. Limit the amount of information per card to aid recall. Practice putting the cards in order until the sequence becomes automatic.

When reviewing new information, copy key points onto a chalkboard, easel board, or other large writing surface.

Make use of the computer to reinforce learning through the sense of touch. Using word processing software, copy essential information from your notes and textbook. Use graphics, tables, and spreadsheets to further organize material that must be learned.

Listen to audio tapes on a Walkman tape player while exercising. Make your own tapes containing important course information.

The Auditory/ Verbal Learning Style

You learn best when information is presented auditory in an oral language format. In a classroom setting, you benefit from listening to lecture and participating in group discussions. You also benefit from obtaining information from audio tape. When trying to remember something, you can often "hear" the way someone told you the information, or the way you previously repeated it out loud. You learn best when interacting with others in a listening/speaking exchange.

Words from the Auditory Learner:

"When I'm taking a test, I can hear in my head the way my girlfriend and I discussed the subject matter when we were studying together. I can hear my girlfriend's tone of voice; I remember at what point we were laughing. Often it is the auditory memories that I remember first—the tone of voice, the laughing. Then I remember the content of what we were saying, and this gives me the answer I'm looking for on my exam. It's amazing to me how strong an Auditory Learner I am. I remember loving to listen to my grandfather tell stories when I was little. My brother couldn't sit still long enough and would always run off before the story was over. But me, I could just listen forever."

Strategies for the Auditory/ Verbal Learner:

Join a study group to assist you in learning course material. Or, work with a "study buddy" on an ongoing basis to review key information and prepare for exams.

When studying by yourself, talk out loud to aid recall. Get yourself in a room where you won't be bothering anyone and read your notes and textbook out loud.

Tape record your lectures. Use the 'pause' button to avoid taping irrelevant information. Use a tape recorder equipped with a 3-digit counter. At the beginning of each lecture, set your counter to '000.' If a concept discussed during lecture seems particularly confusing, glance at the counter number and jot it down in your notes. Later, you can fast forward to that number to review the material that confused you during lecture. Making use of a counter and pause button while tape recording allows you to avoid the tedious task of having to listen to hours and hours of lecture tape.

Use audio tapes such as commercial books on tape to aid recall. Or, create your own audio tapes by reading notes and textbook information into a tape recorder. When preparing for an exam, review the tapes on your car tape player or on a "Walkman" player whenever you can.

When learning mathematical or technical information, "talk your way" through the new information. State the problem in your own words. Reason through solutions to problems by talking out loud to yourself or with a study partner. To learn a sequence of steps, write them out in sentence form and read them out loud.

Appendix C
Learning Styles Inventory

This chart helps you determine your learning style; read the word in the left column and then answer the questions in the successive three columns to see how you respond to each situation. Your answers may fall into all three columns, but one column will likely contain the most answers. The dominant column indicates your primary learning style.

Put a "1" to the right of ALL questions that are a "yes" – even if you have multiple answers on the same row. Total the rows.

The largest score is your preferred learning style. If two or three scores are within 3 points of each other – you have a duo or trio learning style, called a "Combination."

When you..	Visual	Auditory	Kinesthetic & Tactile	
Spell	Do you try to see the word?	Do you sound out the word or use a phonetic approach?	Do you write the word down to find if it feels right?	
Talk	Do you sparingly but dislike listening for too long? Do you favor words such as *see, picture*, and *imagine*?	Do you enjoy listening but are impatient to talk? Do you use words such as *hear, tune*, and *think*?	Do you gesture and use expressive movements? Do you use words such as *feel, touch*, and *hold*?	
Concentrate	Do you become distracted by untidiness or movement?	Do you become distracted by sounds or noises?	Do you become distracted by activity around you?	
Meet someone again	Do you forget names but remember faces or remember where you met?	Do you forget faces but remember names or remember what you talked about?	Do you remember best what you did together?	
Contact people on business	Do you prefer direct, face-to-face, personal meetings?	Do you prefer the telephone?	Do you talk with them while walking or participating in an activity?	
Read	Do you like descriptive scenes or pause to imagine the actions?	Do you enjoy dialog and conversation or hear the characters talk?	Do you prefer action stories or are not a keen reader?	
Do something new at work	Do you like to see demonstrations, diagrams, slides, or posters?	Do you prefer verbal instructions or talking about it with someone else?	Do you prefer to jump right in and try it?	
Put something together	Do you look at the directions and the picture?	Do you like to have someone read you the directions?	Do you ignore the directions and figure it out as you go along?	
Need help with a computer application	Do you seek out pictures or diagrams?	Do you call the help desk, ask a neighbor, or growl at the computer?	Do you keep trying to do it or try it on another computer?	
TOTALS	Visual =	Auditory =	Kinesthetic & Tactile =	

Adapted from Colin Rose(1987). Accelerated Learning. http://www.chaminade.org/inspire/learnstl.htm

Appendix D
Multiple Intelligences Survey
© 1999 Walter McKenzie

The theory of multiple intelligences was developed in 1983 by Dr. Howard Gardner, professor of education at Harvard University. It suggests that the traditional notion of intelligence, based on I.Q. testing, is far too limited. Instead, Dr. Gardner proposes eight different intelligences to account for a broader range of human potential in children and adults. These intelligences are:

◆	Linguistic intelligence ("word smart")
◆	Logical-mathematical intelligence ("number/reasoning smart")
◆	Spatial intelligence ("picture smart")
◆	Bodily-Kinesthetic intelligence ("body smart")
◆	Musical intelligence ("music smart")
◆	Interpersonal intelligence ("people smart")
◆	Intrapersonal intelligence ("self smart")
◆	Naturalist intelligence ("nature smart")

For more information about your preferred way of learning go to
http://www.thomasarmstrong.com/multiple_intelligences.htm

Part I

Complete each section by placing a "1" next to each statement you feel accurately describes you. If you do not identify with a statement, leave the space provided blank. Then total the column in each section.

Section 1

_____ I enjoy categorizing things by common traits
_____ Ecological issues are important to me
_____ Hiking and camping are enjoyable activities
_____ I enjoy working on a garden
_____ I believe preserving our National Parks is important
_____ Putting things in hierarchies makes sense to me
_____ Animals are important in my life
_____ My home has a recycling system in place
_____ I enjoy studying biology, botany and/or zoology
_____ I spend a great deal of time outdoors

_____ **TOTAL for Section 1**

Section 2

_____ I easily pick up on patterns
_____ I focus in on noise and sounds
_____ Moving to a beat is easy for me
_____ I've always been interested in playing an instrument
_____ The cadence of poetry intrigues me
_____ I remember things by putting them in a rhyme
_____ Concentration is difficult while listening to a radio or television
_____ I enjoy many kinds of music
_____ Musicals are more interesting than dramatic plays
_____ Remembering song lyrics is easy for me

_____ **TOTAL for Section 2**

Section 3

_____ I keep my things neat and orderly
_____ Step-by-step directions are a big help
_____ Solving problems comes easily to me
_____ I get easily frustrated with disorganized people
_____ I can complete calculations quickly in my head
_____ Puzzles requiring reasoning are fun
_____ I can't begin an assignment until all my questions are answered
_____ Structure helps me be successful

_____ I find working on a computer spreadsheet or database rewarding
_____ Things have to make sense to me or I am dissatisfied

_____ **TOTAL for Section 3**

Section 4
_____ It is important to see my role in the "big picture" of things
_____ I enjoy discussing questions about life
_____ Religion is important to me
_____ I enjoy viewing art masterpieces
_____ Relaxation and meditation exercises are rewarding
_____ I like visiting breathtaking sites in nature
_____ I enjoy reading ancient and modern philosophers
_____ Learning new things is easier when I understand their value
_____ I wonder if there are other forms of intelligent life in the universe
_____ Studying history and ancient culture helps give me perspective

_____ **TOTAL for Section 4**

Section 5
_____ I learn best interacting with others
_____ The more the merrier
_____ Study groups are very productive for me
_____ I enjoy chat rooms
_____ Participating in politics is important
_____ Television and radio talk shows are enjoyable
_____ I am a "team player"
_____ I dislike working alone
_____ Clubs and extracurricular activities are fun
_____ I pay attention to social issues and causes

_____ **TOTAL for Section 5**

Section 6
_____ I enjoy making things with my hands
_____ Sitting still for long periods of time is difficult for me
_____ I enjoy outdoor games and sports
_____ I value non-verbal communication such as sign language
_____ A fit body is important for a fit mind
_____ Arts and crafts are enjoyable pastimes
_____ Expression through dance is beautiful

_____ I like working with tools
_____ I live an active lifestyle
_____ I learn by doing

_____ **TOTAL for Section 6**

Section 7

_____ I enjoy reading all kinds of materials
_____ Taking notes helps me remember and understand
_____ I faithfully contact friends through letters and/or e-mail
_____ It is easy for me to explain my ideas to others
_____ I keep a journal
_____ Word puzzles like crosswords and jumbles are fun
_____ I write for pleasure
_____ I enjoy playing with words like puns, anagrams and spoonerisms
_____ Foreign languages interest me
_____ Debates and public speaking are activities I like to participate in

_____ **TOTAL for Section 7**

Section 8

_____ I am keenly aware of my moral beliefs
_____ I learn best when I have an emotional attachment to the subject
_____ Fairness is important to me
_____ My attitude effects how I learn
_____ Social justice issues concern me
_____ Working alone can be just as productive as working in a group
_____ I need to know why I should do something before I agree to do it
_____ When I believe in something I will give 100% effort to it
_____ I like to be involved in causes that help others
_____ I am willing to protest or sign a petition to right a wrong

_____ **TOTAL for Section 8**

Section 9

_____ I can imagine ideas in my mind
_____ Rearranging a room is fun for me
_____ I enjoy creating art using varied media
_____ I remember well using graphic organizers
_____ Performance art can be very gratifying
_____ Spreadsheets are great for making charts, graphs and tables

_____ Three dimensional puzzles bring me much enjoyment
_____ Music videos are very stimulating
_____ I can recall things in mental pictures
_____ I am good at reading maps and blueprints

_____ **TOTAL for Section 9**

Part II

Now carry forward your total from each section and multiply by 10 below:

Section	Total Forward	Multiply	SCORE
1		X 10	
2		X 10	
3		X 10	
4		X 10	
5		X 10	
6		X 10	
7		X 10	
8		X 10	
9		X 10	

Part III

Now plot your scores on the bar graph provided:

100									
90									
80									
70									
60									
50									
40									
30									
20									
10									
0	Sec 1	Sec 2	Sec 3	Sec 4	Sec 5	Sec 6	Sec 7	Sec 8	Sec 9

Key:

Section 1 – This reflects your Naturalist strength

Section 2 – This suggests your Musical strength

Section 3 – This indicates your Logical strength

Section 4 – This illustrates your Existential strength

Section 5 – This shows your Interpersonal strength

Section 6 – This tells your Kinesthetic strength

Section 7 – This indicates your Verbal strength

Section 8 – This reflects your Intrapersonal strength

Section 9 – This suggests your Visual strength

Remember:

Everyone has all the intelligences!

You can strengthen an intelligence!

This inventory is meant as a snapshot in time – it can change!

M.I. is meant to empower, not label people!

Appendix E
Critical Reflection on Teaching Practice

Instructions: Reflect on the teaching methods you have used in past classes and answer the following questions ranking the level you practice this method from "1" to "4", "1" being "Rarely or Never" and "4" being "Always."

1 - Rarely or Never   2 - Sometimes   3 - Frequently   4 - Always

1.	Students have an opportunity to connect their prior knowledge to new information.	1	2	3	4
2.	I use quizzes and tests to identify the students' level of learning.	1	2	3	4
3.	Opportunities are provided for social integration and community building in the classroom.	1	2	3	4
4.	Lectures are provided to provide opportunities for students to learn new knowledge.	1	2	3	4
5.	A classroom environment is created for critical dialogue and risk taking.	1	2	3	4
6.	I use fill-in-the-blank handouts and give students the answers.	1	2	3	4
7.	Student work collaboratively in groups on problems that align with course objectives.	1	2	3	4
8.	Students negotiate learning goals and topics for the semester.	1	2	3	4
9.	All the course topics in the course outline are presented.	1	2	3	4
10.	A range of instructional styles is provided to accommodate the range of student learning styles.	1	2	3	4
11.	Rubrics are provided on what it takes to be successful in my class.	1	2	3	4
12.	My personal stories and experiences help students relate to a topic.	1	2	3	4
13.	Learners are able to discuss and apply problem-solving tools to real life situations.	1	2	3	4
14.	Classroom management strategies are used to insure student learning.	1	2	3	4
15.	Topics and materials for students are selected by me.	1	2	3	4
16.	I provide an environment for role plays, case studies, or problem solving projects.	1	2	3	4
17.	Assessment techniques are used to identify the students' level of learning.	1	2	3	4
18.	Reading from the textbook or having students read from the textbook takes place.	1	2	3	4
19.	Students are encouraged to work in groups and learn from each other.	1	2	3	4
20.	I use a computer slide (PowerPoint) presentation in the classroom.	1	2	3	4
21.	Students are encouraged to research additional information on the Internet and to bring questions to class.	1	2	3	4
22.	An effective and energetic presentation style is an important part of my teaching.	1	2	3	4

Critical Reflection Score Sheet

Question	Score		Question	Score
1.			2.	
3.			4.	
5.			6.	
7.			9.	
8.			11.	
10.			12.	
13.			14.	
16.			15.	
17.			18.	
19.			20.	
21.			22.	
Learner-centered teaching style		TOTAL SCORES	Teacher-centered teaching style	

11 – 22 Low Preference
23 – 32 Moderate Preference
33 – 44 High Preference

Your scores may show a mix of low, moderate, or high in both teaching styles. For example, you can have a "34" preference (high) for teacher-centered instructional styles and a "38" (high) preference for a learner-centered instructional style. Scores in this example indicate a preference of using both teaching techniques, with a slight preference toward learner-centered methods.

Appendix F
Class Project - Management Interview

To complete this project, identify a manager that works in a field that interests you. The organization may be a business or non-business organization. Examples of business organizations are banks, retail stores, restaurants, etc. Examples of non-business organizations are schools, churches, governments, etc.

Contact the manager and arrange a time when they might be available for a brief interview. Explain that you are a college student. Be polite and professional. You will find most professionals very willing to accommodate your request.

At a minimum, your interview must cover the following:

> Ask the manager to provide examples from their job duties of activities related to each management function (planning, organizing, influencing and controlling). Give them a brief written description of each to assist them with their answers. What skills do they need for each function?
>
> Do they consider one function to be more important than the others? Which one and why?
>
> What recommendations does each manager have regarding careers in the manager's type of organization?
>
> What do they feel is the most important role of their management position?
>
> What do they know now, that they wish they had known when they were still in college or prior to their management position?

Any other questions that you feel are appropriate.

Summarize your interview in one neatly typed page. Include the name, title, and place of employment of your interview subject. Comment on what you learned from the exercise. You will discuss your results with an assigned team in class and further analyze your results using management theory.

Appendix G
Problem-based Outcomes

Student Learning Outcomes for the skill of Problem-solving using Problem-based or Project-based Activities

Major Skills in Problem Solving Projects
- Thinking skills
- Research skills
- Resource locating skills
- Writing skills
- Display-making skills
- Group-work skills
- Speaking skills
- Self-assessment skills

Secondary Workplace Skills
- Consensus decision-making.
- Diversity appreciation.
- Teamwork.
- Time management.
- Planning and organizing.
- Crisis management.
- Goal setting.
- Flexibility.
- Interpersonal communications.
- Conflict resolution.
- Risk taking.
- Critical thinking.
- Transfer of learning to real world application.

Learning Outcomes - Following instruction and participation student will be able to:
- Identify real world problems.
- Select problems that are solvable.
- Select problems that are appropriate for his or her educational background or experience.
- State the problem clearly and objectively.
- Describe the nature of a problem.
- Select resource material that is pertinent to the problem.
- Analyze and interpret relevant source materials.
- Describe a plan for solving problems.

- List the difficulties of carrying out the plan.
- Describe the process of carrying out the plan.
- Justify the procedures used in carrying out the plan.
- Analyze and interpret the results of the plan and process.
- State conclusions.

Group Outcomes
- Participate in group discussions.
- Make comments that are clear, well-organized, and relevant.
- Ask meaningful questions.
- Listen attentively to the ideas of others.
- Ask questions and make comments that reflect thought.
- Show respect for other group members.
- Complete work assigned by group on schedule.

Performance Outcomes
- Identifying and selecting a problem.
- Locating and selecting relevant resources.
- Writing a report describing the project and results.
- Oral presentation and defense of the project.
- Effectiveness in group problem solving.
- Integrate learning from different areas into a plan for solving a problem.

Class Participation for Problem-solving or Problem-based Activities
- Listens attentively.
- Asks relevant questions.
- Participates in classroom discussions.
- Volunteers for special tasks.
- Contributes materials for the class.
- Helps others.

Values and Attitudes Outcomes – Affective Outcomes
From the book How to write and Use Instructional Objectives by Norman E. Gronlund
- Listens attentively.
- Shows awareness of the importance of learning.
- Participates in classroom activities.
- Shows sensitivity to human needs and social problems.
- Accepts differences of race and culture.
- Attends closely to the classroom activities.
- Completes assigned homework.
- Participates in class discussion.
- Volunteers for special tasks.

- Shows interest in subject.
- Enjoys helping others.
- Demonstrates belief in the democratic process.
- Shows concern for the welfare of others.
- Demonstrates problem-solving attitude.
- Recognizes the need for balance between freedom and responsibility in a democracy.
- Recognizes the role of systematic planning in solving problems.
- Accepts responsibility for his or her own behavior.
- Understands and accepts his or her own strengths and limitations.
- Demonstrates self-reliance working independently.
- Practices cooperation in group activities.
- Uses objective approach in problem solving.
- Demonstrates industry, punctuality, and self-discipline.

Appendix H
Bloom's Taxonomy

In 1956, Benjamin Bloom headed a group of educational psychologists who developed a classification of levels of intellectual behavior important in learning. Bloom found that over 95% of the test questions students encounter require them to think only at the lowest possible level...the recall of information.

Bloom identified six levels within the cognitive domain, from the simple recall or recognition of facts, as the lowest level, through increasingly more complex and abstract mental levels, to the highest order which is classified as evaluation. Verb examples that represent intellectual activity on each level are listed here.

Forming Questions with Higher-Level Thinking Words

1. Knowledge	define, identify, label, list, locate, match, memorize, name, recall, state, tell
2. Comprehension	describe, explain, interpret, put in order, paraphrase, restate, retell in your own words, summarize, trace, translate
3. Application	apply, compute, conclude, construct, demonstrate, determine, draw, find out, give an answer, illustrate, make, operate, show, solve, state a rule or principle, use
4. Analysis	analyze, categorize, classify, compare, contrast, debate, determine the factors, diagnose, diagram, differentiate, dissect, distinguish, examine, specify
5. Synthesis	Change, compose, construct, create, design, find an unusual way, formulate, generate, invent, originate, plan, predict, pretend, produce, reconstruct, reorganize, revise, suggest, suppose, visualize, write
6. Evaluation	Appraise, choose, decide, defend, evaluate, judge, justify, prioritize, rank, select, support, in your opinion

ABOUT THE AUTHOR

Dr. Wendy Flint is Senior Vice President for Boston Reed College in Napa, California and the former Director of Professional and Continuing Education for the Center for Training and Development at College of the Desert (COD) in Palm Desert, California.

Dr. Flint was a tenured faculty member at COD and elected two-term Chair of the Faculty Development Committee. She is the author of several technical manuals including, School Boards – A Call to Action, Instructional Design Methods, Teaching Techniques for Adult Learners, Student Leadership Skills for the 21st Century and Principled and Practical Leadership.

She has presented Transfer of Learning and Problem-based Learning workshops throughout the state of California and was a published/presenter at the 14th International Conference on Teaching and Learning in Jacksonville, Florida in April 2003. Dr. Flint has published in multiple journals on teaching techniques, online assessments and organizational leadership.

Dr. Flint's combined experiences of working in major corporation training departments, including Hewlett-Packard's Ink Jet Printer Division, combined with her higher education faculty experience as a business adjunct professor, brings a fresh perspective to the topic of 21st century learning.

Dr. Flint received her BA in Communications with a specialization in Training and Development from Marylhurst University in West Linn, Oregon, her Masters of Public Affairs from Washington State University, and her PhD in Education with a specialization in Teaching and Learning from Capella University. She is currently working on her MBA.

Dr. Flint resides in Indio, California with her husband of 37 years and three Chinese Shar-pei dogs. She has three married children and six grandchildren.

Made in the USA
Columbia, SC
14 March 2020

89191416R00057